MATTHEW EVANS has been a chef
Until recently he was senior resta
Morning Herald. He was editor of
New South Wales, which sells abc
across the state, and a contributing writer for *The Age Good
Food Guide* in Victoria, which also sells 40,000 copies a
year. He has appeared on television and radio on numerous
occasions, and at one point in his life he ate out on average
ten times a week. He contributes regularly to the *Herald*'s
and *The Age*'s 'Good Weekend'. His latest passion is cooking
at home.

Never

ORDER CHICKEN ON A MONDAY

Kitchen Chronicles of an
Undercover Food Critic

MATTHEW EVANS

RANDOM HOUSE AUSTRALIA

Random House Australia Pty Ltd
Level 3, 100 Pacific Highway,
North Sydney, NSW 2060
www.randomhouse.com.au

Sydney   New York   Toronto
London   Auckland   Johannesburg

First published by Random House Australia 2007

National Library of Australia
Cataloguing-in-Publication Entry

Evans, Matthew, 1966–.
Never order chicken on a Monday.

ISBN 978 1 74166 696 0 (pbk.).

1. Evans, Matthew, 1966–.
2. Restaurants – Australia – Anecdotes.
3. Cooks – Australia – Biography – Anecdotes.
4. Food – Australia – Anecdotes.
5. Cookery – Australia – Anecdotes.
I. Title.

641.5092

Cover design by Nanette Backhouse
Typeset in Centaur 17/14.5 by Midland Typesetters, Australia
Printed and bound by Griffin Press, South Australia

10 9 8 7 6 5 4 3 2 1

Contents

*Writing about eating is like dancing about architecture —
it's a really stupid thing to want to do.*
With apologies to Elvis Costello

I

If the oysters didn't kill them,
the mashed potato should have

TO THIS DAY it still astounds me. It remains a mystery how the restaurant I worked in as a teenager never sent anyone prematurely to their graves. But no-one died: not from the workload. Not from the various forms of human degradation that make up the apprenticeship system for chefs in this country. And not from the knives that flew in the kitchen as tempers flared. Not even from the oysters we served.

There was, admittedly, at least one casualty in that restaurant, when an older bloke choked on his steak and went to the great diner in the sky. His much younger companion was caught on security cameras as she fled the scene, though it's doubted she was a relative or did anything untoward, except excite the old boy too much. That aside, though, I don't recall any other deaths at The Hideously Expensive Canberra Restaurant, where I spent two and half years as an apprentice – despite serving oysters that were on the toxic side of fresh.

It's not a very auspicious start for a food writer of any reputation. To admit to a background cooking food you not only wouldn't want to eat yourself, but shouldn't feed any living thing, is hardly the stuff of a legendary gourmand. As someone who would end up as the chief restaurant critic for *The Sydney Morning Herald*, it's pretty shameful. But as an apprentice at The Hideously Expensive Canberra Restaurant I learnt as much about bad food — how to cook it, how to spot it, and how to get out of making it — as I did about good food. Probably more.

Sometimes we started with great produce and went backwards from there. Australia's sexiest bivalves are the very delicate, indigenous rock oysters, which are best eaten freshly shucked and straight from the shell, never cooked and hardly dressed. Problem was, where I worked, we didn't understand them too well.

When the oysters arrived in our kitchen they were already open, a crime hardly imaginable in Europe. In countries where oysters are understood and loved, to take delivery of opened oysters is akin to receiving a batch of opened champagne. It's not just the wrong thing to do; it's a *terrible* thing to do. Something so delicate and so marvellous should be worthy of royal treatment.

Fecund, sweet rock oysters are lasciviously wet with their own brine, plump and yet never bigger than a man's thumb. They have a flavour boasting equal parts subtlety and complexity as only slow-grown oysters can. Slippery, gently iodiney, they're at once both confronting and utterly desirable, like sex in a shell. But at that time I was still about ten years away from the joyous revelation of fresh, pure, immaculate, just-shucked rock oysters. When my personal epiphany happened, it was thanks to a seafood wholesaler who insisted on opening oysters in front of us, and by that time I was running my own kitchen.

But back in 1985, at work in The Hideously Expensive Canberra Restaurant, all I knew was what I was told. And what I was told looks damned scary with the benefit of more than two decades of hindsight and a working knowledge of bacteria.

Our oysters were delivered in five dozen boxes, opened and washed by the grower, as were virtually every single restaurant's oysters in those days. The gnarly creatures, with their triangular shells curving, always, in a clockwise direction from the hinge to the jagged fringed tip, housed a nugget of meat the size of a teaspoon. They were sandwiched between layers of damp paper to keep them moist. I know now there's no excuse for buying them that way besides laziness and ignorance. While we may have been about 800 metres above sea level, the restaurant was located barely two hours from some of the best oyster farms in the nation. Shame, then, that we completely shafted nature's bounty.

I certainly didn't know any better. I was a fresh-faced apprentice, eager to learn, but green as grass. I didn't even swear back then, and I'd yet to discover the joys of private investigators, tetchy celebrity chefs, defamation cases and spinal surgeons. I'd never enjoyed eating an oyster, despite spending all my school holidays on the coast where they thrived, picking fragments of their shells from my feet and knees after days spent exploring, scrambling over the rocks by the water. When I started work I didn't have any idea what they should taste like, or how they should be handled.

Our oysters were inordinately popular. For one of the city's finest diners, boasting the multiculturalism of a

Greek boss, a German chef and a menu written in French, it was the oysters that usually outsold all other entrees. They outsold the prawn cocktail, most nights. They outsold the avocado vinaigrette, the crepes with chicken and leek bound with mornay sauce, the smoked trout with mango. Oysters were, and arguably still are, one of the most popular restaurant foods in the nation. That's rightly so; when they're good, they're great. But when they're not good, they're scary.

To stop the oysters from slipping we'd lay them on lettuce leaves, the outside leaves from iceberg lettuces (the only lettuce really, in the early 1980s). If the oysters started to dry out on top, which was pretty much inevitable, we'd wash the long dead bivalves in very salty water flavoured with bottled lemon juice. If the lettuce went brown on the edges we'd just throw that out and place the washed oysters on fresh iceberg. For cooked oysters, we'd pipe mashed potato into a circle to help the shells stick to the metal trays they sat on. The trays would then be fired under the intense heat of that amphibiously titled industrial grill, the salamander.

This may have been one of Canberra's poshest and most expensive restaurants, but just because the menu was written in French didn't make it flash. Raspberry sauce for duck breast was crafted by boiling frozen raspberries with raspberry vinegar and cream. We used tinned peaches for the chicken, though we did actually take the peach halves from the can and cut them into fans by hand (like, wow). We'd then dredge the seared breast meat with tinned peach nectar boiled with cream. Frozen blackberries were used in the venison sauce (boiled down with, you guessed it, cream) and tinned demiglaze (brown sauce) and chicken booster (which is something like powdered stock cubes) were used in just about everything. If the fish ever arrived fresh it was usually in bulk so we could freeze most of it ourselves.

That said, the profiteroles were pretty good (even if the filling was made with a bought custard powder rather than from scratch), as was the gravlax, a dill-cured salmon dish that didn't suffer from any shortcuts or cheap substitutes. We even had fresh Canadian salmon before Australian salmon farms came on stream.

We did all right with the critics, too — an indictment on the quality of them more than us, I'd suggest with the benefit of hindsight. In fact, considering what I've seen, and what I know about the way some restaurants treat food, and what chefs are like, it's amazing that I'd ever eat out again, let alone one day become a public palate myself.

Most of the food we served day after day, it must be said, was perfectly healthy. Some of it, maybe even most of it, probably tasted good — especially if you liked sweet, creamy sauces. But amidst the passable, the possibly good, the slightly suspect and the seriously rank, the oysters stand out as the scariest thing I've ever served.

A kitchen team is very strongly bound, at once both as close as a family and as harsh as a gang of convicts. It's a bitchy, high pressure, surreal team of misfits revelling in antisocial behaviour and gross abuses of each other for a cheap laugh. But they also show you the ropes in probably the same way the inmates at Long Bay gaol indoctrinate and teach newcomers how to survive. In most kitchens there was no nice way, no polite way, just the chef's way, where shortcuts, blind fury and physical threats were favoured over proper training and adequate staffing.

Many, many days in this kitchen were busy and there was only one person doing the cold larder section, the section where oysters were prepared. If you got in the so-called 'shit', that poetically titled moment when orders flood in and you can't keep up, there was no way out. Meanwhile customers complained about delays, waiters harangued and belittled us and the meanest bastard of a boss threatened to sack us for the crime, it seemed, of being human. The trick was to get prepared, to have every-thing ready and to 'make it last'.

'Making it last' meant the oysters sat on their plates in the fridge. Some would have spent the better part of three days uncovered, being plunged daily or twice daily in their salty lemon bath. And when they looked overly tired, when the skin on top was so leathery that no amount of washing would bring them back, then of course you couldn't sell them as fresh oysters any longer. That's when you sent them to the hot entree section to be cooked. To be fair, we did smell them to see if they had a fetid odour, but unless it was obvious, and the lemon and salt couldn't hide it, they were still plated as fresh.

As a second-year apprentice who had only recently progressed from the cold larder section to hot entrees up the far end of the kitchen, I often received skanky, long-dead oysters from the apprentice in larder. These were the ones destined to be kilpatrick or mornay.

There was a beaten-up old aluminium ice bucket we used to make up the packaged mashed potato which was piped onto metal trays to hold the oysters in place. I remember the under-bench fridge being so small that usually you couldn't fit the ice bucket into it. So the mash would sit on the bench and dry out, going grey and strangely cracked on the surface. It was reminiscent of a grey riverbed in drought, the potato returning to its flaky, factory produced origins, albeit with a hint of aluminium oxide. But I was told not to worry, the potato wasn't for eating; I just needed to make it last. It didn't matter, because who would eat the thing that merely held the oysters from sliding off the tray, right?

The day sits clearly in my head. I'd been using some of the oldest, mankiest, driest mashed potato ever, which I'd miraculously revived with hot water and beaten with a whisk to make it smooth again, under orders from a qualified chef. We pressed a dozen oysters into it, filled them with mornay sauce and topped them generously with cheese. The tray was grilled and cheese melted down over the side of the oysters as usual. But that day was different, because when the tray came back from the table, the hapless diner had not only enjoyed some of the most dubious oysters in the land, he'd also polished up every last bit of the deadliest mashed potato I would ever serve.

If there's a time in my career that informed me of the good, the bad and the truly ugly in restaurant land, that was it. It's a moment of shame and insight that I've carried through from apprentice to head chef and then later as a full-time restaurant reviewer.

Curiously enough, I still fancy oysters. But these days I rarely recommend them cooked. That's not just because the magical native rock oyster is best when it's freshly opened and served with little except a glass of fizz and a winning smile. It's also because one small part of my brain niggles with the possibility that dubious operators out there are still trying to *make them last*.

2

A first recipe

MAKING VOMIT had been on my mind for some time.

If you hated school like I did, and had parents who thought your only days off should be days when you were actually physically, demonstrably ill, you have to do something drastic. And that something drastic included the first recipe I ever created.

For a family that suffered tragic loss, it was amazing that my parents ever let me out of their sight, let alone were so strict about sickies.

I wasn't always the youngest child. My two older sisters and I had a little brother, Phillip Warwick Evans, who was tragically killed when I was seven. It's something my family hardly spoke about, not openly at least, not until thirty years later when I chanced upon the bridge where he'd been hit by a car at Jervis Bay on the New South Wales south coast. I felt a chill when I first saw the bridge again after all those years, a dreadful sense of loss, a sadness and grief that had not been possible as a seven year old. I'd last seen Phillip there, a trickle of blood falling from the line of his hair before the ambulance arrived. Recognising the bridge triggered family discussions about my brother that my parents couldn't have countenanced when he died, in their grief, their pain. It was a full thirty years after his death that I learnt the details of the accident, and understood why we'd never been back to Jervis Bay in the intervening three decades.

To have a childhood as free as mine after the accident was my parents' greatest gift. Instead of insulating and penning us in, they let us out in the world.

While adults who moved to Canberra during the 1970s used to say that the best thing about living there was that all your relatives lived interstate, the town held plenty of magic for a kid.

Growing up in the nation's capital at that time was a joy. The city throbbed with new arrivals; it had a certain naïve buoyancy, and every suburb had its own pocket of bush, perfect for kids. We scrambled up and down the original Weston Creek, swimming under willows, luring yabbies into buckets with mangled chunks of lamb gristle tied on the end of a piece of string. We watched the advance of suburban sprawl, but never lost our pockets of grassland dotted with trees.

There was the thrill of finding a green patch blessed with plenty of four-leaf clover, which we'd pick and slip between pages of the ancient, brown-bound *Nuttall's* dictionary. There was the magic of discovering birds' nests and wombat holes, the excitement of spying 'roos and rabbits and the fear of magpies swooping down from an impossibly high sky in spring, drawing blood from the heads of unsuspecting cyclists and primary school kids.

My parents must have resolved not to cosset us. To lose their youngest, most vulnerable child at age five to a freak accident must have been unbearable. That my parents let their other children wander the open air, to find their own way at such a tender, impressionable age, must have taken an act of faith that's way off the scale. My parents seemed comfortable to let us explore, with all the risk and pleasure that implies.

We were known in the neighbourhood as that slightly odd family where the kids were expected to be out and about, active until 6 pm. Ours was the family that had a black and white television when everybody else had colour. Not that we were allowed to watch it. My father was so strict about the goggle box that sometimes he'd arrive home and place his hand on the back to see if it was warm. Eventually he gave up trying to catch us out, but still we'd listen for the characteristic squeal of the car's brakes as he rounded the last curve in the street, so we could switch off the telly and be proudly out the back or playing table tennis when our parents walked in the front door.

Dad was the great protector of morals in our household. Television was the bane of his life. Many were the nights when there'd be a communal inhalation from the couch as a couple on the television kissed, only to have us all let out a sigh of relief when it ended. Forget *Number 96*, *The Box* or *Alvin Purple*, even a kiss was risqué in Dad's eyes. He was so embarrassed by things of a sexual or romantic nature, so horrified by crude words, that he made us look up unknown, presumably lewd language we'd used unknowingly in *Nuttall's*, the ancient dictionary that never really deciphered one word without giving you another equally obscure one to explain it. Once you'd started you could spend hours flicking between *archaic, sod, licentious, bugger, vice, moral rectitude, profligate* and more. We were convinced *Nuttall's* only listed words that suggested depravity.

All in all, it was much safer for us to be outside. My sisters and I were not just encouraged to get out of the house, we were expected to be out and about, cruising the streets by bike, skateboard, or scooter. Active bodies and active minds were both parental goals.

Like most of Canberra's new suburbs at that time, all the neighbours had kids around our age – and the local kids shared the streets as a playground. We'd often find ourselves careening down the S-bends that crowned the upper reaches of the local footpath on precariously put-together billy carts, scrambling about in the as yet unfinished houses nearby or just loitering in other kids' garages around the block. We'd get into mild mischief, maybe encouraging Fatty Hall to jump on board my aluminium KISS skateboard, douse it with metho, toss on a match, and then watch as flames peeled off the back as he flew down the impossibly, death-wobbly steep Martens Crescent.

Or watch the flames peel up his legs, as it actually turned out.

Dusk was usually our trigger to head home, to stop catching tadpoles or chasing the fleet-footed bearded dragons that made their home deep in the long grass of Oakey Hill. But dusk was late in the warmer months, and with daylight saving we were often a long way from home.

To get us all to come back to the house at tucker time we had a bell. This ornate dinner bell felt quite large and heavy in the hand, a joy to hold and — especially for a kid — to ring. I believed it was gilt and emblazoned with mythical writing straight from the runes of Lothlorien. In reality it was brass and not really so large or interesting as my childhood memories suggest, but it did possess a marvellous tinkle that had a Pavlovian affect on my sisters and I. You never heard that sound without wanting to get home to the warmth, joy and full table of the perfect childhood.

The entire neighbourhood knew the dinner bell, so if you were too busy shaping pipe cleaners and cotton reels at Street Club, or playing noisy Scalextric cars with a mate, their mum or dad would tell you it was time to head home. The bell had been rung and dinner would be waiting. One time a group of parents decided to show how much they appreciated our evening ritual, and gathered around the house, waiting for mum to cook them dinner.

While it was a brilliant upbringing of carefree afternoons and toasty, mashed potato-fuelled nights, I hated school. Those precious pockets of bushland used to hide me on days when I told the teachers I was going home to eat lunch with mum — despite the fact that she was actually at work.

From the very first day, I'd been disappointed by it. School was, quite simply, dull. School was no match for riding your bike to the river and practising skimming stones. There were no good food smells. You couldn't laugh like it didn't matter or dance without music or climb trees or lick spatulas or steal small squares of dark, strangely compelling cooking chocolate from the pantry. It was books and games of tunnel ball and cursive writing and detention. And foul milk.

Weston Primary, like all schools at that time, made you drink fresh milk that had been sitting, warming, in the driveway for a few hours. Even the teaspoon of strawberry-flavoured Quik that I'd carry to school wrapped in Glad Wrap couldn't salvage it.

School had been built up to be something to look forward to and for the next thirteen years all I wanted to do was get out of there.

Making vomit was to be a minor salvation. To get off school I needed to be sick and have the evidence to prove it. Unlike a headache, which was considered a reason to have an aspirin and put on your school uniform, in our house only actual spew could get you a day off school. I'd seen my sisters pull it off. They, I'm told now, actually *were* ill. But I never seemed to get sick often enough. I had to manufacture illness. Thank you, Australian parmesan.

Making your own chuck chunder, your own barf, ralph or vomit wasn't in any recipe book we had as far as I knew. So I made it up.

I was already pottering about in the kitchen by this stage, making cakes and spaghetti bolognaise and peeling spuds. And I'd already discovered that frying tomato paste made the end dish taste heaps better. Experimentation was part of my upbringing. Dad's training as a chemist meant I had taken test tubes to school full of chemicals that I could make change colour, and I knew the powder to sprinkle on someone's food to make their pee turn red. I'd also shown my fifth grade class that an egg soaked in hydrochloric acid ended up stripped of its shell, leaving a raw egg barely contained by its delicate, squeaky-textured white membrane.

Science, however, only had so much allure. I kept getting drawn back to the kitchen, probably from hunger alone. At one stage I spent three afternoons making nasi goreng, that fabulous fried rice from Indonesia, so I could take it to class for an international day. If that sounds odd for a nine year old, it didn't seem it to me.

Cooking was a part of our lives. We had to eat, someone had to cook it, and typically for the time, a small amount of that responsibility fell to the kids. I just took on more of that role because the kitchen seemed the best place to be.

But chunder was new. It had to be good enough to fool my mother, a woman not known for her lack of attention to the finer points of her kids' upbringing. What I needed was for the spew to be convincing. What I needed was the smell of vomit.

The answer came from an unexpected source. One day I was eating tinned tomato soup. I was thinking: this is okay, but not great. I thought about how spaghetti bolognaise had tomato in it, and tasted better with parmesan on top. (Remember this is Canberra in the 1970s; I'm talking about the pre-grated stuff, the only parmesan that I knew.)

So I took the packet from the fridge, sprinkled it liberally into my soup and began to eat. Problem was, something about the combination had the exact same taste as heartburn. The aroma of that cheese with the acidity of the soup had a kick like chunder. It was so bad that right there and then I almost did the technicolour yawn for real.

The soup was ditched, but the idea for a few days off school had been born.

Whenever my sisters or I felt ill, we'd been told to take an ice-cream container to put by our beds. That way, hopefully, we'd heave into the bottom of a blue Streets container rather than all over the carpet. All I needed was an opportunity.

A few days later and I went to it. My parents slept downstairs, well away from the sounds of the kitchen. So I snuck around at night, squashing some frozen peas, a little tomato sauce, mustard, water, a few bits of leftover meat and carrot, a splash of vinegar and the all-important parmesan cheese. I mixed it all up in the ice-cream container and then left it to fester overnight by the bed. If there was justice in this, it's that I had to smell the offending mixture all night.

The next morning arrived, eventually, and I lay there, long after our obligatory rising time, waiting to see the response.

Mum came in to find out why I wasn't up as early as usual. Trying my best to look and sound crook, I said I didn't feel too well, and that I'd been sick, just a little, in the night. She spied the container, whisked it away and promptly flushed the contents, holding her head away from the offending smell. She was concerned, brought me some water, stroked my brow and asked me if I felt well enough for school. The answer was obviously no.

'You poor boy,' she cooed. 'Well, you'd better not have any breakfast.'

With that I was left very, very hungry. Hungrier, even, than usual. But Mum wouldn't stay home unless I was really crook, and somehow, with the mixture already flushed, I doubted that I'd be sick again that day. So at least I'd be able to raid the fridge when she'd gone off to work. I planned on sneaking spoonfuls of condensed milk from the opened tin, some of the leftovers from the previous night's meal and perhaps one or two bite-sized Violet Crumbles from the packet in the cupboard. But something was telling me that I wouldn't be eating tinned tomato soup with pre-grated parmesan. Honestly, I was never that sick.

3

Hunger is the best sauce

I GREW UP ravenous. I was always hungry. Not that we were poor or that we didn't have enough to eat, but like so many young fellas, I suffered constantly from that aching hollowness that only an active, fast-growing kid really knows. Even when your belly is so full that it hurts, even when you've had third helpings, there's still a gnawing inside. As soon as there's the smallest bit of room you'll be shovelling in another meal or lashings of rice pud.

It's not great to be six foot tall at fourteen years of age. From a hungry, below-average height boy who sat towards the front in his school photos, I suddenly appeared in the back row. From an enthusiastic if untalented soccer player I became the gangliest, most uncoordinated kid in my year. My ribs poked through my skin, you could see my heart beat from metres away, and my limbs did things I never expected them to because they grew too long too fast for the nerves to catch up.

Sure I could pass as older simply by being impossibly tall for my age, but there's only so much joy in drinking vodka lime and lemonade at fourteen years of age in Honey's Discotheque, even if you are wearing brown cords and short-sided brown boots with your favourite chequered shirt.

All this growth and a very active life took an already healthy appetite and made it unquenchable. No wonder that when Dad asked if I'd like to help build retaining walls or change washers I'd be angling to spend time with Mum instead. Like any good cook, she'd often be found making a cake, some biscuits, a hearty roast or preparations for her much-anticipated dinner parties. Hanging around with Mum was the human equivalent of the dog lurking under the table. I'd get plenty of little titbits, off-cuts, samples and tastes as things cooked. I might even get a pat on the head.

My father is a bloke. Not a blue singlet, head-under-the-bonnet kind of bloke, but a man of his time, with firm ideas about what a man should and shouldn't do. As the man of the house, his role was to provide for his family. And a man's role, when I was growing up, didn't involve nancying about in an apron with a whisk. It involved drills and spades and rugby union.

Dad's idea of how I should spend my weekends involved things like cleaning the mortar off old bricks for a cent or two a pop. Needless to say this wasn't anywhere near as interesting as making crepes, cooking pikelets or learning the art of so-called Spanish Rice (which was about as Spanish as Peking Duck). I must have been a great disappointment to him.

And so I learnt to cook when I was young. The smell of a happy home was one where the stove was warm, the biscuits home baked, the cups of tea always 'nice'. My earliest memories are of standing pressed against my mother's legs in the kitchen, the scent of flour, cooked and uncooked, in the air. The smell of my childhood is butter, baked into shortbread or smeared thickly on toast and topped with Seville marmalade. It's the scent of melting cheddar cheese and pork crackling, the fragrance of lemons and freshly mown grass. It's also the smell of peroxide in the bathroom as Mum bleached her hair using weird purple paste. But mostly what I remember is the food, unremarkable, yet good. Amidst the tins of spaghetti and baked beans, the packet gravy and stuffing mix, the curry with banana and coconut, were lard roasted potatoes, runny, vinegary poached eggs on crumpets and the majesty of a multi-layered, impossibly tall Prince Regents torte.

Mum had gone off to work after Phillip died — a way of coping with my brother's death at first, and later a great interest for her when we all had our own lives and our own homes. So we were expected to have the dinner on when she came home, or at the very least the potatoes peeled. And it was always potatoes.

Although our neighbourhood was a mix of nationalities and backgrounds, from diplomats' kids who'd just arrived from the Netherlands, to Indonesians, Greeks, Croatians, Serbians and Indians, and I grew up with friends of all backgrounds who could've shown me plenty about the great tucker available in the world — unfortunately that wasn't to be.

Ours was an unremarkable upbringing of giggling at *The Goodies*, packing death at *Doctor Who*, and the usual dishes appearing with staggering regularity. Tuesday, of course, was spag bol, spaghetti bolognaise night. Wednesday was probably cheesy crunch (or 'greasy crunch', as we called the family favourite of lamb chops baked under a crisp bread and cheese crust). Thursday was stew, variously renamed ragout, braise, navarin, blanquette and daube because one sister decided she hated 'stew'. I learnt a little about menu descriptions even back then. Friday was fish and chips, homemade usually, or fish fingers when we were little tackers. Sometimes it was tinned corned beef, a fried egg and homemade crinkle cut hot chips. I'd beg to be allowed to use the crinkle cut knife to make them. Saturday could be anything, but may have included spaghetti bolognaise soup, a curious and not totally appetising dilution of Tuesday's leftovers. Sunday was usually roast. Grey, dry roast beef or lamb in the tradition of our ancestors, more often than not. And Monday was scraps (called Monday Meats in some households), using roast beef with 'Spanish Rice' cooked in tomato juice, or slices of congealed, dry, cold roast lamb with its fatty, granular texture. Worse still, if there were no leftovers we'd have kidney sauté, a dire combination of pissy-tasting kidneys, bacon strips, tinned corn kernels and starchy boiled potatoes, with no gravy, sauce or attraction. In short, it was food just like most other British immigrants were eating.

My sisters and I made things from a wonderfully large-paged children's cookbook that boasted cute cartoons and a picture of every step in the recipe. I was a dab hand at 2, 4, 6, 8 Cake and roasting popcorn in the big stockpot. Even if I burnt a bit it went to the endlessly ravenous chooks we kept in a pen up the side of the house. They got the peelings, the outer leaves of the lettuce, singed popcorn and other kitchen scraps to supplement their foraging for snails and feed. We got the eggs. I even caught an egg as it was laid once, the light brown orb all soft and wet and warm, almost filling my little hand as it fell.

Maybe it was the era, but we ate pretty healthy food most of the time. Froot Loops were a once a year treat. On road trips, perhaps with our pet chickens tucked into a sack and gently placed underneath our legs, we wouldn't stop to buy meals. The whole rear of the station wagon was designed as a kitchen cabinet, with picnic sets, our own different-coloured aluminium beakers and a gas stove. Food was cooked there, keeping us satisfied, and away from the menacing smells and signposts to greasy chicken or pizza joints (though we did get a huge stash of moist towelettes and a nipple-erasing Colonel Sanders polystyrene surfboard on one trip). Other times we'd have what came to be known as 'congealed bacon fat sandwiches', which had sat in the car for a couple of hours after being made at home. To this day my parents still carry a pepper grinder in the glove box. And bacon sandwiches on most trips.

It wasn't just on outings that they would steer us away from fast food. If the Mr Whippy ice-cream van came scuttling past, blaring Greensleeves from a crackly speaker, we were the last kids in the neighbourhood to know, as my parents would uncharacteristically break into song until well after the van had passed.

Mum did her best. She was probably ahead of her time with the cordon bleu recipes that now look so quaint and dated. I watched in awe during her dinner party preparation as she spent hours slaving over beef Wellington, or 'prawn mould', a cream cheese and prawn dip in the shape of a fish. She never did do a pickled onion and cheese cube 'hedgehog' like some mothers, but there was definitely a fondue or two amidst her repertoire.

She cooked bloody well for her family and her time, considering her upbringing during and after the Second World War. I once asked her what had inspired her to learn to cook, and she confessed that it didn't come naturally, and she certainly didn't learn much at home. Apparently her first two years of marriage were marred by such shocking meals that she couldn't face eating. Dad, probably through a desire to survive each night and remain married, not only ate the food but also wiped his plate clean. Mum could hardly stomach her own cooking. It was a case of either learn to cook edible food or starve. Thankfully for all of us, cooking won.

The thing is, good food wasn't a given. It wasn't expected every day and it was this mentality, a post-war, still-on-rations mentality from the UK, which was passed down to us kids. If we had a block of stilton, it was cherished and savoured, only small amounts eaten at a time, until the cheese itself went just a little manky. (At which time we'd marinate it in port.)

Good food was special. Like the silver cutlery and Noritake china, which only came out for particular occasions, we saved the finest food for best, be it a cheese, halva, fresh walnuts or chocolate. Instead of enjoying every single meal of every single day, we trudged through mounds of starchy grey potato, sawed through tough, dry liver and ate many meals without any tangible sauce or moisture left. Good food, made from pristine ingredients, was meant for a celebration or guests. It was accepted, culturally and within my family, that everyday food could – and often would – be mediocre.

When Mum was entertaining things did look up, but there could still be an austerity to the meal, especially if you were family. We even had our own code when there were visitors, so we didn't overindulge. FHB, meaning family hold back, was whispered to and between my sisters and I if we didn't have enough food on the table to satisfy all the kids, both parents and a guest or three. Hospitality ruled, and guests were treasured.

Even when there were no guests, as grommets we knew our place. As the head of the house, Dad was always given the baked custard dish to scrape out. He'd sit at the end of the dining table and meticulously scratch at every little bit of caramelised milk that had baked onto the side of the baked custard basin. Dad was allowed to pick over the chicken carcase, and he was always offered the treasured parson's nose. He sat at the head of the table, carving roasts, getting more of the nutmeg scented skin (fly's walk) on the rice pud, doling out the ice-cream and generally doing things a man of his generation did. Not a lot of cooking, but some heroic eating when called upon.

We were always well fed, despite the occasional dry or dull meal. Every night we'd sit together as a family, the table laid by one of us in turn, complete with our own serviettes held in wooden rings with a coloured band so we knew whose was whose. We used the serviettes for a few days in a row, each of us required to eat neatly and sedately, folding and rolling them at the end of the meal ready to be slid back into the wooden rings for the next day.

Food was fuel. But gradually I began to discover some things that tasted fantastic. Sugar could be caramelised toast under the grill to make a buttery sweet treat. Marshmallows were a favourite, roasted over coals so the outside went dangerously dark, the lava-hot insides molten and gooey. I discovered that the pan where the pork was roasted had a brown sludge in the bottom that tasted like roasted pork times 1000.

It wasn't just at home that the revelations came. My paltry pocket money, supplemented by an income earnt cleaning mortar off bricks, was in danger when I started high school and had to walk past the corner shop on the way. It was thrilling to stumble across Pop Rocks, a sweet that fizzled and crackled deafeningly on the tongue, but which came scarily close to choking you if you swallowed too much. There was the strange soapy taste and texture of musk sticks. The best value seemed to be in Wagon Wheels, chocolate-coated biscuit sandwiches that appeared to be about as big as my head. There was endless excitement in discovering other novelties: hard lemon lollies filled with a mouth-tingling buzz of sherbet; sugar-coated jubes; salt and vinegar chips. We'd buy Redskins on the way home from school, bags full of milk bottles, cobbers, caramel buds and freckles, or *twenty cents' worth of mixed lollies please sir. No liquorice thanks.* I eventually found that square, bite-sized Violet Crumbles weren't as racy as Crunchie bars.

At the school tuckshop I discovered the wonderfully nicknamed 'snot block', aka vanilla slice, a custard-filled pastry topped with teeth-rattlingly sweet white icing. When I was given fortnightly lunch money, most times I spent it on 'rat coffins', those marvellous named-for-a-school-boy meat pies. We'd plunge the pointed squeeze-bottle tip into the middle of the searingly hot pastry lid and make sure the pie filled with ruddy, sweet tomato sauce. I ate mine by peeling off the top and spreading the sauce evenly through the meat, invariably scorching my mouth, my fingers and sometimes my bare legs with dropped filling in the process.

At barbecues with real Aussies (rather than recent imports), I discovered why they call snags 'surprise bags' and would loiter around my parents to try and snare a chop or a sliver of their steak instead of the pale, fatty, dubiously smooth-textured sausages in charred casings that were fed to the kids.

In many ways my childhood was close to perfect, evidenced by the fact that my sisters loved the chocolate stripe in neapolitan ice-cream, which left me to enjoy the strawberry and vanilla. Of course the container was always useful if you felt sick in the night, too.

On the day I hit fourteen and nine months, the legal age, I started work. It was a part-time job on the local milk run, and for an energetic boy one form of heaven. At first I was paid three dollars for about ninety minutes of running; lugging glass milk bottles to the front doorsteps of every house in my suburb. The white crate held twelve 600 milli-litre bottles, each with its colour-coded foil top. I'd clasp the crate in one hand, legs pumping and lungs screaming, as I climbed the hill to deliver six gold, the unhomo-genised stuff for the big family at number 10; two red, the homogenised milk for the young couple at number 14; and two blue, the rarely seen low-fat milk, plus a straw-berry Moove flavoured milk for the flat-roofed place at the end of the street. It was terrific fun for a boy with too much energy, an outlet better than sport because it paid. And such princely payment.

A few months later, for a reason I no longer recall, though a bit too much energy to burn may account for it, I started a second job working at a grocery store in a mall fifteen minutes walking distance from my house. Between the two jobs I was often out working four evenings and one day a week. Add that to five full school days – and talk about hungry when I got home.

The only relief came from the supermarket bakery where the smell of freshly baked buns, even those that were bought in as frozen dough and ended up as virtual poly-styrene, puffy and tasteless, was irresistible. They filled me up for at least an hour at a time.

Each night that I was on the milk run, dinner was cooked and plated as normal in my absence. Mum would put the covered plate over a pot of simmering water to keep it hot until I arrived home, which looks quaint, now, in the era of microwaves. But it worked like a dream.

If my mum was the cook and inspiration, my father was the kitchen klutz. Sorry, Dad, if you read this, but you know it's true. Such was his regularity in burning the crumpets under the grill that I began to think of that charred crumpet smell as the scent of a loving home. The bloke can build a house, in fact he did build the first house I lived in, which is pretty impressive for a man who qualified as a research chemist rather than a brickie or chippie. But put him in a kitchen and he's not comfortable at all. His movements become tentative, his mood one of apprehension.

Dad's culinary skills extended the full gamut from crumpet-scraping to bread-scraping. Vogel loaves, sliced bread full of what I think of as gravel (but is actually multigrain), filled our freezer so we'd never be without bread midweek. The stiff frozen slices were relatively easy to prise from one another and Dad seemed to relish his role as maker of lunch. There was a rhythmic scccrrr, scccrrr as he forced margarine onto the rock-hard slabs, much as if he was attempting to butter a coarse tile. Topped with compressed chicken, or maybe a curiously bread-sized square of ham, but with no relish, salad, cucumber or tomato, these dry, rather unpalatable sandwiches fuelled my parents through the days. Popped into old bread bags (complete with a million stale crumbs that then clung to the bread as it thawed), they indirectly paid for my unremarkable middle-class upbringing through frugality alone.

Not that I had to eat Dad's sandwiches. I'd long been responsible for my own lunches. When I first started school I used to keep the occasional lunch money and hide behind the kindergarten, telling the teachers that I was going home for a meal. Of course I got sprung, and not only for that. Like most kids, I secreted food that didn't please me, and plenty of old, mouldy sandwiches were discovered in my Globite school case over those early school years. So from quite young I was told that there would always be bread in the house, and there'd always be toppings and meats. But because I'd wasted food, I'd have to show how much I wanted lunch by making it myself.

Eventually I did make my own lunch, but the best pickings were usually someone else's. I'd take sandwiches offered by those ungrateful kids whose parents had put salad or pickle or multiple slices of juicy, real corned beef on them. When I did take lunch it was more like a picnic, with buttered bread, chunks of gouda, carrot and celery sticks and some fruit. I found moist sandwiches with tomato or cucumber or salad became soggy by midday, and most other sandwiches were too dry. So I'd stack the lunch box with a resilient, flavoursome European style bread, some of it honeyed, plus a slab of emmenthal, a whole ripe tomato and a chunk of cucumber that I'd eat like fruit.

At school, everybody had to do at least one term of home economics. The best thing for a teenage boy is that cooking class meant you left the room with a bag full of Chelsea buns, or lasagne – or at least a belly full of tucker. The blokes who ended up choosing woodwork in later years came out with a pencil case and sawdust up their nostrils. Those in tech drawing got ink on their hands and the prospect of a high-paying job. But we ate well and ate lots.

At school, as at home, we had to eat everything on our plates. You couldn't just throw out food, and an ability to eat everything was highly prized. Years later it would make me fat, but as a nipper it just left me with a great sense of the value of food, and a slight disdain of leftovers. We actually had 'Use up Scraps' nights, as I've noted, where all the old bits in the fridge became dinner. Sometimes it was a great dinner. Sometimes not. At any time you could ask for seconds, but you had to eat it all.

Food, the cooking of it and particularly the eating of it, loomed large in my psyche. Growing up in an inland city meant that I was never going to be captivated by the surf. I was too much of a dag to be a skater or popular. I dressed like I was a scientist in the CSIRO or had got up in the dark, and as for ambitions, they were all pretty modest. I didn't want to change the world one restaurant at a time, or even one meal at a time.

There was no depth of culinary history in my background, no prosciutti hanging in the garage, no amazing Greek Easter or rare pig breeding. There are no professional cooks in my family that I know of, apart from a second cousin, no gourmands of note, and certainly no celebrity chefs. I didn't set out with ambitions or goals.

All I knew was that I wanted to feed people for a living. Not that I was a food groupie. I didn't have posters of chefs on my walls. I'd never heard of celebrity cooks beyond Britain's wonderful lush Keith Floyd, camp entertainer Bernard King and Mr Cheese, Peter (G'day) Russell (G'day) Clark. But I did like the idea of being paid to do what I adored. There was an impossible-to-overcome gnawing inside me to produce something with my hands that was tangible, edible and maybe even incredible. And by the time I was in my last years at school, I'd decided I was going to be a chef.

All I wanted was a good life, a good meal from time to time, my health and a few close friends. Cooking eventually took my health, my friends, my social skills. It did earn me a modest living and gave me more incredible meals than it's possible to count. But while great food was my inspiration, the reality was starkly different.

I didn't know it back then, but I was about to step into a world untouched by many modern concepts, such as sexual harassment laws, sick leave, manners or even good food.

From the minute I entered the dark heart of restaurant kitchens, life as I knew it altered forever. I learnt the importance of working fast, with the immediacy of feedback you very rarely receive in other work. I saw first-hand the power and intimacy of a closely knit team. But I struggled to come to terms with the people I met, the things I saw. There truly was evil in the world. I spent eighty hours a week with some people who were vile human beings: people you would cross continents to avoid, people you wouldn't trust to put fuel in your car, let alone food in your mouth. And they worked alongside me, cajoling, sneering, schooling us apprentices in their foul-mouthed, foul-breathed, Neanderthal way.

All this was unimaginable if you came from my background. My family didn't just pretend to get on well; we actually did enjoy each other's company. Harsh words were rare, arguments brief, and people didn't typically shout and throw things. It wasn't quite Huckleberry Finn fishing trips and Boy's Own Adventures, but it wasn't far from it. I grew up free to roam, eyes wide to the wonders of nature, of travel, of cultural diversity, but I was also emotionally cosseted. It wasn't the best training ground for the destructive storm that I was about to enter.

Sure, I'd heard a few tales of how hard the industry could be, but I had run a marathon at fifteen, and I'd been at the bottom of the pay scale since starting work part time. All the talk of hard yakka and antisocial hours didn't dissuade me. I'd been working weekends and evenings for most of the previous three years, and the thought of joining the public service, where most of my schoolmates were heading, filled me with angst. I didn't want to be bored at work. I didn't want to go to parties and brag about how lazy I'd been all week, or spend my days watching the clock. What's more, call it madness, call it naïve, call it utter stupidity, but I desperately wanted to cook for a living.

In contrast to the current shortage of chefs (Australia is estimated to be about 2500 qualified chefs short at the time of writing and it's expected to worsen in coming years), in those days getting an apprenticeship was hard work. You had to sell yourself.

In the 1980s, you had to get approval from the apprenticeship board before you could look for a job. They checked your school records then sent you a list of restaurants and other institutions (hospitals, hotels, clubs, even Parliament House) that were approved to train apprentices. I went through the list and sent about fifty letters with my rather short CV.

I received three replies: one polite decline and two bites from potential employers. Before I made up my mind I worked a few nights in one restaurant, Chez Arrogance, let's call it; a cramped, explosive kitchen with an abusive French chef. He made superb sauces . . . and my skin crawl, as he touched up a school-age waitress and spat venom in his thick accent.

There didn't seem to be as much cooking going on as reheating. Not as much fine food as greasy meals and Olympian-standard Gallic indifference. I'm sure the chef was pissed most of the time, if his slurred speech, blurred vision and incomprehensible ranting were anything to go by.

I couldn't believe this was the world of restaurants. It seemed too tawdry, too spiteful, and too aggressive for an industry where the front of house is so hospitable. In hindsight the restaurant probably was no different from most places where hubby cooks and the missus serves, and the food did have some integrity. For me it was just like another planet, and one I didn't want to live on. If that French chef did nothing else, he helped in my decision to opt for a bigger kitchen.

As I finished school, hoping to enter a world where you could be paid to cook, I had no true concept of what lay ahead, the hours, the kind of people I'd meet, the opportunities that would one day come my way. Cooking certainly wasn't the usual career path in a government-dominated town and certainly not one that my dad, the first in his family to get a degree, considered appropriate.

My father took me to one side in the weeks before I started my four-year apprenticeship. He explained that while he'd support me in anything I wanted to do, cooking for a living was considered rather effeminate. When I wondered aloud what that meant, he told me to look it up in *Nuttall's*.

4

That Old German Bastard

'BOY!' THE WORD is bellowed, short, sharp and with piercing intensity.

'Yes Chef.'

'BBOOYYY,' Chef yells again with frightening aggression, even though I am less than a metre from him and he must have heard my reply.

'Yes, Chef,' I reply once more in a mouse-tiny voice, using the polite 'Chef' form whenever I address him, even though he's introduced himself as Fritz. As a first-year apprentice, I was the Boy, and he was – and always will be – my capital 'C' Chef.

'Let me tell you zis, Boy,' Fritz commands, his middle-aged, steak-red cheeks bulging under his surprisingly clear, dramatically blue eyes. 'Never, ever, no matter vot else you do,' he rails, waggling a not insignificantly sized index finger close beside my face, 'never, ever, EVER, become a chef.'

It was curious advice to be given by your mentor, a man you're considering indenturing yourself to for a four-year apprenticeship. It was even more remarkable because this was the first morning of my first day working for this monolithic, foul-mouthed, frankly quite scary German chef. All decked out in my crisp, new white jacket and regulation clogs, a week after finishing high school, I was feeling pretty excited about my first full time-job, and this wasn't what I expected. Was it an omen? Nothing about the hospitality industry ended up being what I'd expected.

Virtually every day of my first year the banter was the same. 'What should you never do, Boy?' Chef would ask with hypnotic regularity.

'Never become a chef,' was the reply he demanded from me, or any of the apprentices loitering in the kitchen at the time.

This was Fritz's way of saying that he was bored, that cooking had been good to him, but that there may be other ways of earning a living where brutal heat, razor-sharp knives, undiscerning guests and a cheapskate boss weren't the norm. It was Chef's way of warning us, three boys and one girl, that the industry we had chosen was full of danger: physical, sexual and emotional. That restaurant owners wouldn't want to piss on us if we were on fire; that we'd be underpaid, overworked, and treated like human waste by a brigade of antisocial misfits and deviants. It was his way of having a laugh at our expense, of making his days pass quicker, and ours too if we weren't on the receiving end of his jibes.

Fritz was in his forties at that time, and apparently a much milder man than in his formidable youth. He'd mellowed, I was told. It's a frightening thought, Chef as a young man.

For Fritz, a laugh was worth having, even if it hurt someone. In fact, it was probably better if it actually did hurt someone. Watching an apprentice lose balance and disappear head first into a chest freezer and not re-emerge would have him cackling so hard he couldn't stand.

The laughs also flowed freely from seeing fingers nicked and gouged while learning the finer points of knife technique, even if he was always conscious of our wellbeing. In my second week, I sliced part of a knuckle off and nearly fainted with shock, which put him — though thankfully not me — in stitches. The funny part in hindsight, though I still bear a small scar, is wondering whose oysters kilpatrick the offending skin went into after it was lost in the mound of bacon I'd been dicing.

Fritz's jokes knew no cultural, sexual or tasteful bounds. When the baker refused to deliver on a Saturday because he was Jewish, Chef uttered the dreadful words 'vee had a solution to zat problem,' in a particularly menacing tone under his breath in what could've been a thicker than normal German accent.

When he sneezed and you didn't say *'gesundheit'* he berated you for not caring.

'So vot's zis?' he'd chide. 'No "bless you", no *"gesundheit"*? Just vot are you sinking? Zat I hope zat old German bastard just falls over and dies?' he'd exclaim, looking seriously affronted. 'Is *zat* vot you sink? You ungrateful fuck.'

Was he joking? Was there a gleam in his eye or did he look like he'd implode? Fritz, if nothing else, was enigmatic.

Along with his assertion that you shouldn't be a chef was the assertion that you should 'never, ever, EVER, employ a woman. So help me Got.' Yet he employed at least three female apprentices that I know of and a few others in the kitchen in various sections. Go figure. And he certainly had a notable feminine side himself.

Fritz loved to rile the apprentices, but he rarely confronted the chefs, a ragbag crew of half-trained sloths masquerading as black-and-white clad professionals. He'd slag off 'zat lazy fuck' who expected the apprentices to do all his prep. The feared despot of a leader was our mentor and partial protector from this dodgy, nearly-criminal element who got away with things no other workplace would countenance simply because they wore chequered pants. Fritz was our sounding board, but not our saviour.

For all the fire and brimstone, for all the foul-mouthed abuse, almost perversely Fritz often provided some sanity in a business that spits out far more apprentices than it qualifies.

Yes, Chef did play a knife game where he'd pin an apprentice's hand to a chopping board, spread the fingers and use the tip of a boning knife to find the board between each joint. The idea was to get faster and faster without drawing blood, but he never really got up to speed, and to the best of my knowledge never cut anyone.

Yes, he did call me a *schleim scheiße*, a slimy shitter, most days, though he did it with warmth and a glint in his eye that allowed me to forgive him. Almost.

And yes, he did say 'you all dig your own fucking graves, you dickhetts,' in frustration when none of us four, pale, stressed-out apprentices took his advice. He was trying to arm us against the unscrupulous owner of the business, whom I will call Con; the 'Black Widow' manager; and the cowboys who called themselves chefs. But we admired and – some of us at least – actually liked the grey-haired tyrant nonetheless.

One of the lessons I learnt from Fritz was that

everybody has to earn respect, they aren't just given it. A VIP? 'Just another dickHETT' Fritz would spit disdainfully when asked to give preferential treatment. A politician, a supposed gourmand, a friend of the owner's family? 'Zey're just another dickhett to me,' he'd say. And mean it. Not that he was better than them, but in Fritz's world nobody was better than anyone else, and to do your job properly was to do it *properly* rather than just doing a decent job when somebody, supposedly more important, is watching. We learnt that all customers deserve the same, the best you could put out within the constraints of where you worked. Nobody got special privileges, nobody was treated any differently. Unless it was your family, in which case you might know their tastes intimately and cook accordingly.

All the time, while teaching us, arming us, protecting us, Fritz played the fine line between managing us and keeping us interested. All of it done in a characteristic chef kind of way, a mix of dangerous humour, foul language, a disdain for pretension and with a handful of testosterone-fuelled fury thrown in, crushing some in the process.

As apprentices, despite his barbs, we adored him when we didn't hate him. Maybe it was Stockholm syndrome where prisoners fall in love with their captors, but our strongest feelings were usually of resentment rather than hate. We even, unusually for the restaurant world, bought him a present. Christmas isn't a very holy or particularly festive time in restaurants, what with the 100-hour weeks and the seemingly insatiable public. After the two-month lead up, starting at Melbourne Cup day and finishing after New Year, most chefs can barely speak coherently or remember where they live let alone be cheerful about a mythical man in a red coat. Working Christmas day doesn't fill the hardened convict element that works in kitchens with joy. But we did, begrudgingly, acknowledge the season among ourselves. Seeing as Fritz thought we called him the Old German Bastard behind his back (it was actually far worse), we decided to order a large new knife – F Dick, a German brand of course – emblazoned with those very words. Chef's 'big dick', it predictably came to be known.

While not old, Fritz did have a few years on most chefs. He acted as chef-manager much of the time and didn't usually do the plating of meals during 'service', that manic time between noon and 3 pm and again after 6 pm when diners actually order. At The Hideously Expensive Canberra Restaurant the kitchen was divided in two; a large preparation kitchen in the basement, and a narrow, airless service kitchen much closer to the restaurant itself. Fritz would work downstairs, arriving early in the morning, preparing the raw meats and the seafood. In fact most everything from base sauces to salad dressings and cakes were made in the basement, and only the final cooking of ingredients was done upstairs. Chef would usually have one or more apprentices to help him and keep him company; often the younger apprentices, so he could teach them the ropes and prepare them for the cyclonic effects of service and the malicious intents of the staff. We'd race him at boning out chicken, flying through the dull jobs so we could take his work from him, learning as we went.

Upstairs was where we were sent to work with the mean, usually incompetent and often fiery lesser chefs. It was in this kitchen that most of the frightening things happened to the food – and to us – away from the watchful eye of the Old German Bastard.

It was up in this kitchen, when it was busy, that the excitement and seemingly impossible task of putting out a meal every few seconds balanced the mind-numbing drudgery of dull jobs and slow nights. It was service that provided the true experience, the rollercoaster ride of kitchen work. Upstairs we learnt to work fast, to answer straight away, to accept our failings and successes immediately. We learnt to make things last, to churn out food at pace. I was forced to eat a big bowl of yellowing lettuce one day after I served some to a customer, to prove just how bad it was.

The cold larder section is where a restaurant's cold entrees and salads are served, the traditional place where the first-year apprentice learns to plate up food, to keep track of their dockets – the things orders are written on – and organise their fridge. It's the training ground for just about every chef serving a tuna carpaccio, wagyu beef steak or tomato tarte tatin today. Even in some of Australia's most expensive restaurants, the cold larder section is still run by apprentices. Think of that next time you find grit in your $12 salad.

I was taught to keep up with orders by being prepared. *Mise en place*, a French term meaning everything in its place, was a buzz word before we even knew the term buzz word. Everything had to be ready for the mayhem of service, that scary time when you may be called on to dish out eighty entrees in an hour. *Mise en place* meant an orderly array of pots and bowls, full of cut up garnishes, finished sauces and washed lettuce that allowed you to pump out the food with minimal effort. If you ran out of anything, you weren't just in trouble, you were in deep, deep shit. Especially with the restaurant's owner, Con, who didn't want explanations. He just insisted you never, ever run out.

'Make it last,' was the maxim. To run out of food was the ultimate sin. To water down a sauce, thin a dressing, fine, if you could get away with it. If we were running low on crumbed fish for the fisherman's basket, we'd beat chicken breast out thinly so that nobody would be able to tell the difference (and we never received a complaint). But to run out? You'd be berated at best, abused at worst. 'Making it last' helped the chef's bottom line. It helped Con buy a BMW and send his kids to private school. 'Making it last' was the kitchen's way of saying 'we're good, we're organised, and we're not going to be outsmarted.' It was also a way of saying that you don't give a flying fuck what the food tastes like, or how fresh it is, just so long as it doesn't run out. A smaller than usual portion size? Who cares, as long as the waiter doesn't end up having to apologise to the next customer for being short on a dish.

When we were busy, we prepared everything ahead. Not just lemon wedges and slices of crocodile terrine. We didn't just delicately 'fan' avocados and julienne raw beetroot as a garnish. Some chefs pre-seared steaks for busy nights, and microwaved the chicken stuffed with bug meat so it was cooked through and only had to be browned in the oven. As apprentices we splashed the curling, dry-edged brown bread and butter triangles with water and laid a wet tea towel over them to freshen them up. We'd pre-make pots of 'champagne' sauce with cask white wine and cream, thickened with arrowroot. We also readied oysters, traying up dozens and half dozens of fresh molluscs ready for the heat of service.

For all the downsides, the work was thrilling. It was equal parts excitement, dread and anticipation each night as we prepped our sections ready for service. When the dockets flooded in, as orders and the occasional knife flew, when chef and apprentice alike barked requests, it was exhilarating. Cooking became less important than surviving. The artistry of plating up the meal became second nature as dish after dish left the kitchen to feed the masses. When we were busy there was a tangible buzz in the air, an excitement like I've never felt in any other job before or since. Shame, then, that so many others in the kitchen had little respect for themselves, let alone us, or the customers.

One kept touching the end of his dick, as if checking it was still there. Sure we were all accustomed to 'chef's crotch', the itchy rash bred from constant 40 plus degree heat, but this bloke was obsessed. Often he'd come to work drunk and managed to burn pretty much everything. There are plenty of alcoholic chefs out there (where Fritz trained they had to lock the almost unconscious chef in the toilets each afternoon for three hours to dry out). Most hard-drinking chefs cook better when sozzled, but this bloke was an exception. The apprentices, as usual, saved his skin several times a week.

This kitchen was mild compared to many. We never saw the fish delivery bloke with blood pouring through his hands after being king-hit by the chef, as happened at Melbourne's finest French restaurant at the time. There were no assault charges against anyone here, unlike a later restaurant I worked in. We did recycle butter after it had been on the tables, but not like one posh hotel in England did. The butter dishes sat next to the ashtrays and after a couple of glasses of Bordeaux, so I was told, the punters would get their co-ordination wrong. The butter ended up studded with cigarette butts, yet was still scraped into the recycle pot at the waiters' station.

Our chefs never once punched the apprentices, as far as I saw. Yes, a little intentional burn, the occasional bump so they'd cut themselves, and some pretty serious emotional trauma, but nothing outright. I don't believe the knives that came my way were pegged directly at me. Usually it was more inadvertent as they glanced off benches or boards where they'd been thrown in frustration.

That wasn't to say we weren't threatened. There was plenty of bullying and intimidation. Sometimes even Fritz would roll his sleeves up mid-argument, but none of us was prepared to take up his invitation to step outside and settle it. He was big, and probably quite handy with those massive, grapefruit-sized fists that thumped down on the bench as he berated us daily.

Kitchens are full of danger even before you add other chefs to the mix. What with the knives, the heat, the slippery floors and the infectious diseases spread by the floor staff, it's hardly the kind of environment you want someone who's emotionally unstable to be let loose in. But kitchens seem to attract those wild-eyed, coked-up hospitality vampires who despise daylight and cultural norms. They also attract the kind of people who would electrocute themselves if they were an electrician.

I watched as the insecure, wretched 'qualified' chefs

belittled waiters for their own amusement, grabbing them in anger and frustration and, at least once, banging a waiter's head against the other side of the pass that separated us from them, into the nails that held the paper dockets in place. Everything we learnt about staff training, about management, about personal skills and appropriate behaviour at work, we learnt in an environment of aggression, tension and fear. It didn't set us up very well for a future in the business, or in life.

There is a certain militaristic hierarchy in a kitchen. It works because you can't dither and question orders when you've 140 mouths to feed in an hour. It's a hierarchy that pervades all kitchens, though rarely put as succinctly or as honestly as during my time as a first-year apprentice. 'First comes the Chef,' Fritz would say, gesturing with his hand raised high in the air to show a scale as he spoke. 'First comes the Chef,' he'd repeat, 'then a long time nothing,' as he moved his hand lower and lower to show how much anyone else mattered. 'Then here,' he'd say with his hand nearly at the bottom of an arc, 'comes the Chef again. And maybe, just maybe,' by then he'd be gesturing at the floor or thereabouts, 'down here somewhere, maybe, comes you.'

At least we knew our place.

I was a sensitive soul compared to many. My childhood didn't prepare me for the dark undercurrent of terror that I encountered at work; some of us don't need to have our throats grabbed to make us listen. Delicately phrased statements like 'Fuck off, arsehole' – one of the milder taunts in a kitchen – were never heard in my childhood, and especially not from someone in a position of responsibility. The scariest thing that ever happened when I was a kid had to do with the Daleks, a cushion and the couch. And although I toughened up quickly – on the surface at least – in among the excitement and buzz of the job, I did find it hard going.

Some people coped much better. The apprentice we'll call Umblefumble, for instance, took unprecedented abuse. Being told to 'fuck off, fuck off and die right now in front of me' merely made him shrug, and his capacity to never learn from his mistakes was legendary. Because even the smaller abuses that I took left me smarting, and I could feel it eating away at my self-esteem – when I had the time to think about it – Umblefumble's ability to ignore it all was pretty impressive. I was envious, although not of his incredible clumsiness.

Umblefumble's forearms were always plastered with blisters garnered as he took pans from the oven or salamander and grilled his flesh. He cut himself so often he had to provide his own first-aid kit. To work next to him – and believe me, you work right under the armpits of everybody else in a kitchen at some point – was to put yourself in danger. He'd scorch your hand as you helped him plate main courses, a frypan straight from a red-hot stove pressed down onto your knuckles as he stumbled through service. For all I know he's out there right now, cooking dinner and burning some apprentice's hand tonight.

Not all the burning and bumping was accidental. The chefs used to heat the plates under the grill to see just how much skin they could take off the waiters' fingers if they picked the plates up without a cloth. Ditto for frypans that the kitchenhands grabbed from the end of our trolleys, the handles purposely made so hot that they'd melt through the dish pig's rubber gloves in an instant. It was mean, spiteful behaviour designed to belittle and possibly hurt. And we found it funny, though I cringe when I think about it today.

Waitresses were groped, apprentices too. I was sexually harassed well before I'd heard the term, by those who didn't take a no as a no, let alone a knife raised in anger. Chefs threatened to slit our throats. To fuck us up the arse. To make us squeal like pigs. It seemed like only yesterday that I was ambling home from school and the worst thing that could happen was kicking so many stones up the footpath that I'd end up with holes in my Bata Scouts.

Thing is, even amidst this chaos, the antisocial banter, arse grabbing and often scary food, I loved it. It wasn't doing good things to my head, but I *adored* cooking, and I couldn't actually believe that I got paid to do it. Cooking and this weird, parallel world were actually scarily addictive and often terrific fun, so my first pay packet of $102.70 for the week seemed like a bonus. It was 1984, and money went further then, but every week we had to buy a knife or some other tool for our kit. We had to supply all our own knives and uniforms, with no allowance other than our pay. My first purchase, a small paring knife (Matthew's Little Dick, as Chef predictably called it), cost $25, the second one, a cook's knife, cost $42. Luckily after paying tax of $2.70, then forking out for board, buying and laundering uniforms, purchasing safety shoes, textbooks and tools, the rest was ours to live it up. Fritz helped us out; thanks to a punishing roster we didn't have much of a social life to spend it on.

'Don't plan *anysing.*' That's what Fritz always said. And he meant it. If you want to be a chef, don't plan anything and DON'T, whatever you do, get a girlfriend. If you ever had the good fortune to snag a weekend evening off, the phone could ring and you'd be filling in at work for some joker who had decided they didn't want to work any more some time between lunch and dinner. Of course they wouldn't have told anyone, but when a chef doesn't show up for a shift, they've moved on.

For all the suffering, long hours and emotional black-mail, by rights an apprentice should expect good training. But so much of what I know about good food didn't come from that time.

It was at that first restaurant that I learnt to make a lime sauce using bottled lime cordial boiled down with cream. In fact I never saw a fresh lime in my entire apprenticeship. The ginger sauce was made with Stone's Green Ginger Wine boiled down with, ahem, cream. The sorrel sauce hadn't been within cooee of real sorrel (and I didn't see or eat sorrel for another twelve years). It was at The Hideously Expensive Canberra Restaurant that we used a quite foul-tasting packet mix to make the white sponge cakes, although to be fair the chocolate sponge was a work of art, eggs whipped into almond paste and scented with the finest Dutch cocoa.

It was Fritz who showed me how to make demiglaze – a brown sauce correctly made with veal stock and caramelised flour – using a dark brown powder from a tin, yet also how to make a very good mushroom soup. He told us that caviar was a waste of money and that truffles were overrated. The black tyre-like substance that we pulled from a tin, called 'truffle substitute', certainly didn't taste good to me, let alone look that nice. It was so compressed that it had the shape of the can embedded in it; more Michelin tyre than Michelin star. Once shredded, it was set into aspic on the top of pâté, or folded into terrines. On one occasion a customer complained, saying that our 'truffle' wasn't the genuine article. We were unnerved, and in awe. Someone in our restaurant had actually tasted real truffle.

Often even the simplest of dishes were compromised, and this at a restaurant boasting one of the finest menus in town. Fritz's pancakes were legendary; he'd work three or four pans at a time, pulling one pancake after another from the heat, lining them up on the marble bench to cool. But we must've been on a cost saving measure because instead of a decent number of eggs, he'd use just a few and boost the golden colour of the crepes using 'egg yellow' food colouring. When Umblefumble decided to copy the technique one day while the chef was away, he turned them a radioactive golden hue with a dodgy pour of the food colouring. And we still sold them.

To call Fritz's pancakes 'crepes' is perhaps a trifle flattering. These were thick, rubbery, pale discs that could be thrown like a Frisbee when cold, and tore when you tried to fold them.

I don't think most chefs are artists. Most, like Fritz, are simply tradesmen, just doing a job, but for a lot less money than a plumber or carpenter and with shit hours. The techniques are easily learnt. It takes no passion, no burning desire, no creativity, just plain old grunt and marks too low to get into another course, or social skills too lacking to stay in a real job. Other, better chefs are craftspeople, who take those well-known and trusted techniques and hone them to produce things of great beauty and form. And just a few, the rare and precious few, do novel things with flair and artistry that also manage to taste fantastic.

This last group, however, wasn't part of my early experience. We looked on horrified as our chefs spat on steaks, or stamped on them with their foot and threw them in the deep fryer as payback for customers asking for them to be cooked well-done. 'Peasants,' they'd say, as though we weren't peasants ourselves. I was there when Con, the restaurant owner, crumbed a cockroach into a schnitzel, deep-fried it, and served it. By accident, of course. Over time, the appalling standards started to eat away at staff morale.

One Sunday we started a carvery, with the intention of emulating and possibly improving on the home-cooked Sunday roast. On the first Sunday, fresh meat was roasted then checked to make sure the cuts were moist and succulent.

On the second Sunday, the leftover roasts from the previous week were defrosted then heated in the microwave for over fifteen minutes, still wrapped tightly in plastic film. You could bounce your way from Sydney to Perth on them. 'Roast' potato and pumpkin were actually steamed then plunged into the deep fryer, the same fryer that cooked fish, scallops, and those boot-indented well-done steaks, as well as deep-fried oysters. We cooked cheap pasta well beyond al dente, rinsed the flavour off it, kept it warm in the bain-marie for up to three hours and served it with awful meat or tomato sauces which had no resemblance to Italy's.

As an apprentice, I only knew puff pastry from a packet. I believed that duchess potatoes, mashed then piped into rosettes (the epitome of *haute cuisine*, obviously) were supposed to be dry and starchy and not very good to eat. Our version of Strawberries Romanoff was made using cochineal food colouring and a cheap and nasty cooking liqueur, because Grand Marnier or Cointreau were too expensive. This in a flagship restaurant in a city of over 200,000 people. But it was all I knew.

One of Fritz's specialties was known to us as Old Boot Soup. Everything went into the biggest stockpot. Bacon trimmings, ham bones and plenty of onions joined dried beans, vegetables that didn't look like they'd make it through another day, and virtually anything else. In some commercial kitchens and homes it's known as 'fridge soup' after the fact that you pretty much empty the fridge into the pot. In our kitchen, though, it was Old Boot. The Chef was known for his clean-out frenzies. Old boots would go missing from the changing rooms with disturbing regularity, and kitchen legend had it that it was the missing boots that gave these great, meaty, beany soups their grunt.

Fritz's soups were generally very good, particularly his creamed soups — even if they do seem a little rich in hindsight. But mistakes were never thrown out. A burnt soup, one where the cauliflower had scorched on the bottom, was flavoured with curry and salted heavily to take away the smoky flavour. It didn't work and for days we took it upstairs but warned the waiters not to sell it, eventually throwing it out, as it formed an inevitable crust over more than three hours in the bain-marie.

The food was often bad but I don't entirely blame the

Chef. Cooks work inordinately long hours in a blistering environment. They serve the food they're told to or are expected to by their bosses – and the tighter the budget, the more burnt cauliflower soup they slosh out.

Customers are the ultimate barometer, and we got away with serving slops every single night with very few complaints. If customers are happy paying big money for third-rate meals, and a restaurateur can make money from it and provide employment for chefs, where's the problem? Fritz could really cook, given time, a decent budget and an audience that cared. Most chefs are as discerning as their audience, or as good as their boss wants them to be. And our boss and audience didn't seem to care, so neither did we.

Despite the increase in the quality of dining in this country over the last couple of decades, the kind of food we served when I was an apprentice is still being served in restaurants around Australia today. And that doesn't give me confidence.

While I wasn't the world's best apprentice, I probably wasn't a complete dud, either – not that I'd know it from the feedback at work. Sure, I'd done well at TAFE, but being told you're great '…when you're asleep', or that 'even a blind chicken can find a corn' – apparently a German saying meaning that any idiot, if they thrash around long enough, will do something right by accident – did start to wear thin by the time I'd completed my first year. High praise was 'you're not a complete dickhett,' the emphasis firmly on 'complete'.

The sanity in my world, in those spaces when I wasn't working, also became my downfall. I was a long distance runner, and between split shifts (the two shifts that define lunch and dinner, about 9.30 am to 3 pm and then again from 5.30 to 11 pm) I'd be training. It was a hobby I could pursue at any time, alone, regardless of shifts. It helped me let off steam, to refocus, to relax. There was a moment of clarity during each run, a feeling that the world made sense. It was addictive, I realise now, thanks to the endorphins it released, providing a tremendous feeling of euphoria that I'd seek to revisit often in life.

Running gave me far more joy than working with many of the chefs and I threw myself into it. It reminded me of my carefree childhood afternoons. On a Wednesday I'd be pounding the pavement doing a sixteen kilometre training run. On a Thursday morning I'd run for an hour, then work five or six hours, go to the track and run for another hour or more, then back to work for another five or so hours. My body, and my brain, started to implode.

As the running added to my exhaustion, the other chefs began spending a lot of time doing some serious demeaning. In my first year I'd been called 'The Boy' by all and sundry, a not always critical term, in fact one that almost felt like endearment by the end of the year. But on hitting second year, a new first-year apprentice became The Boy, and one of the chefs decided to call me Crap Head, a name that I never did warm to.

It seemed Fritz, too, was intent on making life hell. Along with his usual rants and mind games, he started a new diatribe with unfathomable origins.

'YOU,' he'd yell out, for no apparent reason, 'yes, YOU, you little shit.' A curious way to talk to someone just shy of twenty and nearly two metres tall, but it was the way we were accustomed to being spoken to.

'You know vot, you stupid fuck? You'll never, ever make a chef.'

I had a holiday booked, no time and no self-esteem left to deal with the barbs, and suddenly I seemed to have little of the passion which had coursed through my veins most of the year. For sixteen months I'd worked as hard as I could, trained like a demon, and endured a pay packet that left a lot to be desired. I was, in fact, burnt out, which is easy to see in hindsight, half a lifetime later. At the time I was just utterly broken.

For months I'd been on a downward emotional spiral at work, as my self-esteem plummeted. Eventually, I pulled the ripcord.

'If I'll never make a chef,' I told the Old German Bastard one day in April, sixteen months after starting work, 'then I quit.'

Fritz didn't speak to me for the last two weeks. Not even to say I told you so.

After quitting my apprenticeship I went travelling. I sat on hilltops in Nepal, outside brasseries in Paris, supped on the true pizza in Naples, all the while dreaming of food: what I'd like to do, how I'd like to do it.

But instead I worked in an office. I worked in insurance. I went to uni, studying mostly sports science and nutrition. At university, I was among people passionate about every topic from alpine plants to architecture and felt the infectious nature of their drive. I was struggling to feel the same passion for the work I was doing, but food was still a major focus for me — even though I'd become a vegetarian for a while after a run in with bad mince.

I fell for a girl who cooked like an angel and was passionate about food. She was always on the prowl for the perfect coffee, the perfect yoghurt, the best real Chinese restaurant. As a shift worker, she still managed to have a life, showing me that perhaps I could manage it too. Lynn understood good tucker, but wasn't involved in the madcap world of hospitality, so I imagined she'd be a voice of reason and could see it for what it was. She gave me the confidence to dream of cooking once again.

Five years later to the month, one Bachelor of Applied Science in the bag and some dull jobs under my belt, amazingly — stupidly perhaps — I still wanted to be a chef.

I'd been obsessed with food, the cooking and eating of it, for the intervening five years. It wasn't just a matter of finishing something I had set out to do. I sensed there was a world of food out there that I had yet to learn about. An apprenticeship would be my ticket to learn about the world through the food it eats.

But first I had to go back to the drudgery, the hours, the chefs and the restaurant owner I'd rather not share a table with, let alone oxygen. But there was no choice. I had been a drop-out and had to prove myself doubly worth taking on. So I was prepared to put up with the barbs, the often appalling food and Con, a man who threatened to sack any of his staff who dared speak to a union official.

I had to swallow a lot of pride to go back to the same restaurant, to the same Old German Bastard, and ask for work. At first I crawled back in, offering to work for no pay, to get my skills back. Fritz eventually warmed to the idea and sacked another chef to get me a job. His overly polite manner, however, was a sign that he didn't trust me, or indeed like me. When the vitriol, spite and humour returned a few months later, I knew I was back in the fold.

Fritz was happy to have me back, but he also knew I was older, a bit wiser and that he couldn't get away with quite as much as before. The same couldn't be said for Con.

When a potato croquette, a crumbed log of mashed potato, blew up in the deep fryer with my arm above it, it coated my forearm with searing hot oil. My immediate reaction was to wipe it off, a cloth in my left hand used to smear boiling oil down to my hand. The skin bulged and blistered from my elbow in an arm-wide teardrop shape, narrowing down near my wrist. A blister the size of a peach filled with fluid; soon after, the skin popped and peeled back like wet tissue paper. Through all this I kept working with an ice-packed tea towel strapped to my arm. When Con heard about it, he asked the chef who witnessed the accident, 'are you sure he's not just making it up?'

When I became a third-year apprentice, after two years in the job, I was informed that because I was on such good money (the princely sum of about $6 an hour) it was time to take the responsibility of a qualified chef. We may have been on a low wage so we could afford to be trained, but this place ran on the labour and skills of apprentices much of the time. Check out the age of the person who cooks your next restaurant meal, and half the time they look like they should still be at school. Being given responsibility is flattering, but without the cooking skills and more import-antly, management skills, these kids burn out well before they should. Unscrupulous operators constantly screw up young, ambitious, passionate chefs well before their time, and the industry suffers from it.

After a year back at work, I complained about excessive unpaid overtime to our restaurant's pay office — there was always some, but this went too far — so when another chef acted on it and went, secretly, to the government-run arbitration board, it was me who bore the brunt at work. I was considered a troublemaker because I'd learnt not to take as much crap as some of the others. It was just an age thing, though in this case it didn't work in my favour. First Con told me to take a week off without pay because he couldn't 'afford my wages'. And then most of my pay was docked for an 'overpayment' they'd mysteriously discovered from the Christmas before, which swallowed any back pay from the unpaid overtime. And I never did find out what the overpayment was.

By day and night I'd be slopping out whatever food was expected of me, but sitting in the car in between shifts (or at Gus's wonderful café on the cusp of Canberra's centre, Civic), I'd started reading food magazines. I had discovered real restaurant reviews, the kind that appeared in national magazines, which introduced a whole new level to my food world. In *Gourmet Traveller* I read about restaurants where quality mattered. Finally my belief that there was brilliant food out there, somewhere other than in this restaurant, was vindicated. I found informed, accurate, inspiring writing that used criticism as a tool to empower the reader. While *Gourmet Traveller* never seemed to review any places that I could visit in Canberra, I was inspired to try and visit the places it *did* review one day, and I subscribed after reading a single issue.

Thanks also to *The Sydney Morning Herald*'s exciting, opinionated (if at the time somewhat pompous) 'Good Living' section, I could sense the existence of a parallel restaurant scene out there. There actually were restaurants where the fish wasn't frozen, the vegetables didn't come from a bain-marie, and the deep fryer and cream sauces weren't the standard ways of cooking just about everything.

I started to read about real restaurants that blew my mind with the dishes they served and the ingredients they used. And I knew I had to get away from Con's place before my passion for cooking was once again knifed into submission. After giving nearly three years of my life to the Old German Bastard and a boss who could barely remember my name, it was time to move on. Though that second time, importantly, I left with Fritz's blessing.

5

A chef's life?

'GOOD AFTERNOON, shithead,' said the chef in a tone so sarcastic it could cure salmon. It was 8.45 am after the previous night's one am finish and I'd thought it was early enough for a nine o'clock shift. The chef thought differently. 'Nice that you could deign to drop in,' he added, icily.

Nobody told me cooking for a living would be like that, although perhaps by now, with three years' experience under my belt, I should have worked it out. Turning up to work early wouldn't be early enough for most chefs. Half an hour ahead of time is usual, almost expected. Fifteen minutes early is late by most kitchens' standards.

When a morning started like that, it'd be eyes to the list and knife to the board for the next two hours before the chef would even speak. Nobody else in the tight-knit team would be brave enough to gesture within sight. You would stand, or fall, without as much as a sideways glance from the rest of the brigade.

Probably – thanks to the telly – cooking for a living is not the great unknown now that it was for me. That said, there are still a lot of things they don't show you on *Boiling Point* or *The Naked Chef*.

For a start, being a chef is an incredible privilege. Being paid to cook, working with a finely honed brigade in the pressure cooker of a commercial kitchen, pumping out hundreds of meals and running close to the wind is a joy only another chef would know. It's a heady ride, the thrill akin to a rock climber's, overcoming insurmountable odds to get through the shift. Nailing service with a closely bound team is euphoric, even if they are a ragged mob of deviants and outcasts hardly fit to socialise with in the rare moments between sleep and work. Glassy eyed, scorched, nicked, bleeding and stinking like a sardine's crotch, the chef at the end of service is no pretty sight or smell. But they know a pleasure like no other.

What the careers counsellor doesn't know about is all the stuff the industry isn't proud of. The assaults and worse. The emotional games. The vitriolic abuse that can sprout up at any time, for no apparent reason. They don't tell potential chefs about all their overtime disappearing at the flick of a pen as the boss fills in their time sheet. They won't tell school leavers that chefs are so well known by number crunchers that they'll be labelled as high risk for everything from insurance to loans. The romance of working a cruise ship or island resort is never accompanied by warnings about STDs and alcoholism, drug abuse and Gambler's Anonymous. Then there's the divorce rate, the suicide rate and the health problems from the mostly nocturnal, hard-working, hard-living lifestyle.

Of course it's not all downside. Some cooks do have a great life and still retain some dignity. Many don't scorch their brains with too much coke. Not all chefs grope you, come at you with a knife or abuse you for their own kicks.

There are those who pay properly and treat their workers with respect. Some of those might, if you're extremely lucky, cook good food.

The sad fact, however, is that most restaurants in this country still serve crap food and apprentices could well spend all their useful waking hours, for several years, learning how to cook it. Those that escape the mediocrity can still end up mopping floors as a head chef several years later. Somebody has to do it and the quicker all the work is done, the quicker a chef gets home to their loved one (if they've managed to find a loved one, and keep them).

A chef's workload, at first glance, is just like you'd expect, only bigger. Any sizeable kitchen has a mountain of preparation to do. Cooks may peel garlic for four hours under relentless fluorescent light. Or spend a day in an airless room chopping fiery chillies until they bleed through their skin. It happened to me. Where I've worked, apprentices often ended up washing pots because the boss was too cheap to pay a kitchenhand. At others I was buried under ten hours' worth of garlic bread learning nothing about cooking, or running a restaurant, but a lot about the human spirit and lack of compassion. Legs ached, arms ached, fingers ached. Eventually they went numb.

Tight staffing numbers mean most chefs don't call in sick – not even if they have made their own vomit. They can't leave a team of three – the usual small-kitchen-restaurant brigade – with one person down. Chefs work when feeling like crap. They work until the job is done. They push their bodies and brains into territory few other professions demand. Cooking isn't surgery or law, but you need to have your wits about you, and a whole different set of skills, when you've got to put out a hundred meals in an hour and you've just come down with the flu.

Timing is everything, though even the monotonous jobs have to be done at pace. At posh places, all those podded peas, the carefully boned fish, the wisps of optic-fibre-width kaffir lime leaf – that, dear reader, has all been hand-cut at speed. Good restaurants spend hours taking the little shoot from the inside of garlic cloves, pressing wafers of filo between metal sheets to cook them perfectly flat and finely shredding green onions. It all sucks up time, and until a few years into it, maybe for your whole career, it's all your time.

This work is often done in split shifts, one focusing on lunch, the other on dinner, with a break in between. In our bigger cities many chefs work what's called a double shift. A double shift is kind of like a split shift, except there's no break. That could mean a start of 9 am (or 8.30 if you're good) – and you'll finish when the work is done, probably close to midnight, though it does depend on the neigh-bourhood and the place.

The higher up the ladder you go, the more responsibil-ity you have, and the longer the hours. Most head chefs are there when their staff arrive, and still there when the team leaves. It's the top tier of chefs that do the ordering, most of it phoned through and left on an answering machine in the wee hours. Sometimes it's done very early the next morning. I know a chef who talks to his fishmonger at 6 am each day, even before he speaks to his partner.

Deadlines define a chef's life. There's one chance to cook each meal and get it right. If it's wrong, the only options are serving the dish knowing it's buggered, or making the customer wait while you cook another one. If there are three immaculately seared whiting fillets waiting for other people on the same table, cooking one dish again is not an option.

A kitchen in full flight is much like you've seen it on television: tempers flaring as often as flames in the pans; waiters being abused; apprentices being called all manner of names. Like an athlete, however, most of a kitchen's time isn't spent in front of the cameras at peak performance. Most is spent preparing for the rush. In the kitchens where I worked, the chefs would use much of the week to build up supplies and prep ready for the madness of Saturday.

For many restaurants, particularly outside the centre of bigger cities, that one day on the weekend can be as busy as the rest of the week combined. Tongs are spun around fingers in quick-draw, Wild West fashion. Hands fly, pans flick and flitter, eyes dart around and brains go into meltdown trying to keep up with all the things that are cooking at once. In this scenario, chefs become like dancers in a tightly choreographed scene; cooks gliding past each other gracefully at speed, whisking like demons, razor-sharp knives passing effortlessly through meat, beautifully arranged dishes pumped from a space smaller than many domestic kitchens.

At its height it's a beautiful sight. At its worst, it's a nightmare of dropped pans, singed meats, customer complaints and a few nasty burns for you to lick before the whole shitfight starts again. All this pressure breeds anger, or if the kitchen is already angry, it amplifies it.

Added to all this work, the demands of the job, the strict hierarchy, the crack-induced paranoia of your work-mates and the all-pervasive nervous anxiety, you can add another factor. A kitchen is unbearably hot; close to 50°C in places, especially next to the stoves, where you have beads of sweat running into your eyes and your undies. The advice on my first day was 'don't drink, that way you won't sweat'. It was fine to dehydrate yourself dangerously, but not to have salt stinging your eyes.

Curiously, despite the pressure, worse than the busy days and nights, far worse, were the morale-crushing slow days. It was on quiet nights, when squalls and freezing temperatures or a big footy game kept people in their homes, that we went a bit stir-crazy. Where I trained, these were the nights the martial arts expert would practice techniques. On us. 'I'll show you how much body control I have,' he said to me one day. 'I can throw a punch and stop within millimetres of your face.' Only he stopped millimetres after hitting my face.

He'd also sharpen the arrow blades for his hunting bow until they shaved hairs off my arm. On quiet nights we'd stand around finding people to pick on, the blanket of boredom settling like a fug over our heads, the food we cooked staler and made with less care because we had to be dragged from cricket games in the loading dock, or from cooking curries for ourselves. Short, intense periods of manic activity were spaced, irregularly, with mind-numbingly dull times when you had to stay at work, sometimes with three cooks to serve two people.

If you become a cook there'll be nights when all your mates are at the pub and you're standing around talking to dimwits about their cars, their latest rash or pig hunting, desperately waiting for service to start so you can escape. While you're on low wages learning how to cook bad food, the IT dork you had better marks than at school is buying a Ferrari, shagging girls, travelling to Europe to ski and not working a single night or weekend. You may spend Sunday night peeling spuds or crying over a mountain of onions, waiting for customers who never show, while your school friends bond over a barbecue.

For many chefs, those pale, stressed-out, haggard orcs of the industry, a social life could be the smoke at 'lunch', possibly at 5.30 pm after eight hours of work. Mine sometimes consisted of a late-night beer, lurking at the bar of the same restaurant where I'd just cooked, attempting to befriend a waiter I had told to shove a pumpkin up his arse only an hour before.

Some nights I'd skulk around after work with other apprentices, most of them pale, dog ugly, pierced and tattooed. We didn't look like the rest of the population, more like a gang of bikies – though without the charm or confidence. By the time we'd put in our paid hours, unpaid hours and the unexpected extra shift or two, there was only so much pep left in most of us.

Often, apart from the other chefs, and the waiters, who I'd try hard not to resent, the only other people I formed any kind of relationship with at work were the delivery men. As an apprentice, TAFE – an acronym for Technical and Further Education – was a respite from this world, a welcome break from the limited number of people you meet in a kitchen.

As trainees we were as harsh on each other as our chefs

were with us. We'd belittle each other, scaring most other groups of trainees as we moped around tech college: a gangly, pimply, thuggish mob clutching our tall hats, trying to crack onto the hairdressing students, drinking at lunchtime and thinking up derogatory names for each other. 'Hey Lobster,' we'd yell out to the red-headed apprentice, a man who earned the nickname not because of his hair colour, but because his head was full of shit. (When you cut open a lobster, the head is full of brown, mucky, smelly stuff. It's actually called 'mustard', and can be used to flavour sauces, but generally it's considered to be shit.) Geronimo got the name from his habit of scratching his arse (the old childhood chant about cowboys and itchy-bums). Any chance we had we'd put down those around us. It was, after all, the way we'd been taught.

TAFE training is an obligatory part of an apprentice-ship, and many bosses hate it. After all, they're paying wages while you're not at work. In the first year we went full-time for twelve weeks, and in years two and three we went one day a week during the school term. Often we'd have to go straight to work after tech, so a relative bludge of a day turned into something more like a twelve-hour shift.

TAFE was supposed to show us skills we didn't learn at work. In many ways it did fill gaps, but they taught us some pretty old, dated and disgusting ways, too.

Chinese class involved boiling sugar and vinegar with tomato sauce and cornflour to make sweet and sour pork, without any reference to a reputable Chinese chef or the cuisine proper.

French classics involved plenty of nods to *Escoffier* and peeled grapes, and you'd lose 10 per cent of your marks if the grapes or the requisite chopped parsley were missing.

We learnt that the public was so gullible that not only could we keep calling silverbeet 'spinach' but we could cut the hard centre out of each leaf, steam it and coat it in a cheesy mornay sauce and call it 'fennel' gratin.

In fact, the local TAFE was full of bad ideas. My personal favourite was how to make staff meals cheaply from a 'raft', one of the byproducts of consommé.

A consommé is a very flavoursome stock that is clarified so it is as brilliant as a diamond and glistens like a glacial brook. To clarify it you use minced meat (beef for a beef consommé, chicken for chicken, and so on) mixed with egg whites and usually some vegetables such as leek, carrot and celery. Stirred into a stock and brought to a simmer, the mince and egg mixture rises to the top. This mix pretty much vacuums up all the crap as it drifts through the stock and floats to the surface to form a firm raft. While it cooks, the flavour from the mince is drawn out into the broth, along with the flavour of any vegetables. So the raft is left with little of its natural flavour, and lots of dead blood cells and other scum from the broth.

Our teacher taught us to make meat patties for staff meals from it. If you could find something more full of all the impurities from food, and without the actual flavour of its ingredients, I don't know it.

The teachers varied in quality. One told us that cheap cuts were peasant food, that if you could afford to, you should just eat fillet. Presumably because he didn't know that fillet has the least flavour of any cut of meat.

You couldn't call TAFE a proper benchmark. I never saw a vanilla bean in my three years at tech. I never saw a lime.

The tomatoes were as hard as cricket balls, the seafood rarely fresh. I certainly never learnt to open an oyster.

There's a massive difference between the front and back of house that shocked me when I first started cooking. The soft muzak, the gentle reflected lighting, the carpet, excellent paintwork, clear-skinned staff who smile, they all disappear when you hit the kitchen. In there it's all recycled air, harsh edges, scuffed paint, onion farts and jokes landing on the wrong side of obscene. Outside the swing doors are the customers, inside are the chefs, and those who work between the two, but mostly in the calm dining room, are the waiters.

Like their pirate brethren in the kitchen, most waiters are a breed apart. Many seem to just enjoy being hospitality junkies, hiding from the world, in love with the late starts and late-night shenanigans. Many are uni students. Many are not waiters, they're actors, so *there*. And some, a rare few, are professionals like you've never seen.

A good waiter knows that the young couple on table 3 don't need anything in a hurry; they're just too into each other to care. Give them a drink and keep your distance.

The good waiter can tell that the older couple on table 26 are in need of some entertainment. Conversation died some time in the 1970s, and they want drinks, food, and an all-singing, all-dancing kind of service straight away.

Waiters, those shiny restaurant staff that can talk to another human without swearing, often unwittingly piss off the chefs. A predominantly casual workforce, they breeze in, get paid more than the cooks, work half the number of hours and have a real, outside life (which they tell the cooks about, innocently, and in detail). It's hard not to resent them for it. My social life, particularly early in my career, was usually sitting around between shifts listening to some drongo chef talk about petrol siphoning and the problem he had with crabs. The other sort.

I've worked with a range of waiters, from the smarmy and obnoxious to the charming and inspired. I've worked with people who are so pedantic about the look of their restaurant that they'll pounce on a customer who has moved his cutlery and put it back where it ought to go. Others, though, are *all* about pleasing the customers.

'Do us a favour and do that button up,' we naïve teenagers used to say to one forty-year-old waitress who exposed to the world a neck line that plunged more than we thought possible.

'No chance,' she'd say. 'This one button is worth an extra hundred dollars a week in tips.'

I've worked with people who made my skin crawl, lazy bastards you'd want to sack if you were in a normal job, smash in the head if you were a chef, and whose hygiene left a lot to be desired, but who were nonetheless terrific with people in the dining room. Go figure.

Despite their owlish lifestyle, most waiters, by the mere fact they have to face the public, usually do fit with many of society's norms. If a waiter rides a bike to work, they're probably getting fit. If a chef rides a bike to work, they've probably been done for drink driving.

Kitchens have changed in some ways since I trained, but the bullying, the antics and the lack of proper training continue to plague the industry. While there are now many restaurants that don't degrade and belittle staff for sport and that cook delicious food at the same time, good, hard-working chefs drop out every single day, unable to cope with the madness.

Years after my apprenticeship, over 60 per cent of chefs still leave the profession within five years of starting their training. (In a 2005 report on the industry in the Northern Territory, it was noted that out of an average of sixty trainees each year, only nine complete the training.) That means most never see full wages, let alone enjoy the benefits of travel, recognition and perhaps celebrity that can sweeten the job.

Many of those who survive are hardened hospitality trolls that don't see daylight, who know and care little about good food and even less about human relationships. Some use a little pharmaceutical help to get through the day and focus their mind for the rush of service. But for most, the long days become long months, the long months drag into years, and we've now got a culture of kitchens where very few chefs can, or want to, work past forty years of age. There's a destructive element to the industry that does nobody any favours. The lost knowledge and expertise alone is criminal.

Character building? People in the industry use this as an excuse, to be sure. But that's just crap. It's possible to be a good person and a great chef without the dinosaur attitude that dogs the industry. I've even met some. The explosive, abusive, spiteful world might make it seem a sexy profession to some diners. It might make terrific television to watch somebody being mistreated and belittled, but it sure as hell makes it a profession in need of a few more souls. It's not hard to see why we're thousands of chefs short of demand. There's a whole generation of chefs out there who have been abused and will abuse.

The images I grew up with, of the hotel chef in his starched fluted hat, of a rotund and jovial Paul Bocuse walking around French markets chatting to stallholders – it's not real. Being a chef isn't about showing up with a surfboard and a camp stove at idyllic locations. It's more like being a cross between a cleaner and a machine. You're the battery hen of workers: kept under unnatural lights and forced to produce until you cark it. It's about being the bloke on the European bus holiday that everybody expects to cook each night. It's being the girl who has to fight ten times as hard to survive in a testosterone-driven kitchen as her male counterparts, coping with lewd behaviour and dangerous advances. It's a mostly tough, occasionally rewarding, sometimes scintillating job that doesn't resemble any other in modern times. And it's a great profession if you can handle it.

I can't complain. I've done pretty well from the industry. I can't say I've made a fortune from it, but cooking has afforded opportunities I never dreamt of when I first pulled on the clogs and chequered pants back in 1984. The price, however, from the long-term injuries to the break-down of relationships, is not one I'd want to pay again.

6

Backbreak Hotel

POP.

It didn't sound like much. As I leant back over a brat pan, a supersized, floor mounted, deep frypan set below waist height, to take the weight of two pork legs and their accompanying steel tray, there certainly was a sound. Curiously enough, I didn't feel any pain, not even in the base of my spine where the noise originated. What really concerned was not only the POP, but also a wave of nausea that left me woozy. No sting or ache, just an eerie, dizzy silence.

Psycho Chicken, as the section chef was known for his unpredictable, flighty and pretty frightening behaviour, slapped the side of the oven with his fist, and said that one day someone was really going to hurt themselves here.

By that time, someone already had.

The pop I'd heard in front of the oven wasn't just a sound. I'd felt sick for a reason. One cartilage disc in the base of my spine had slipped – 'herniated' is the correct term – and my bottom vertebra had split into three parts, two bits cracking from my spine, one lumbar vertebra shunting forwards. For a long time I thought this was how my life would fall apart; not with a bang, but with a pop and a whimper.

I'd come to a new job as keen as curry powder. This was One of Canberra's Swankiest Hotels. It was supposed to be my salvation from the mediocrity of The Hideously Expensive Canberra Restaurant. I'd heard a lot about how this hotel had set the benchmark in terms of quality. From the time Con at The Hideously Expensive Canberra Restaurant had told me – as a still very poor apprentice with rent to pay, a car to run and the usual life expenses – that he couldn't afford my wages and to take a week off without pay, I was on the prowl for work. I contacted One of Canberra's Swankiest Hotels by letter and phone. I met with the executive chef. I spoke with people who had worked there who, mostly, had good things to say about the quality of the place. I then rang the chef every week, pleading shamelessly to be given a chance.

Getting a job this way was a humiliating process but the thought of wasting the remainder of my apprenticeship learning more bad ways to treat staff and ingredients wasn't thrilling. Added to the difficulty of getting out of my contract at Con's restaurant was the fact that I knew other places could be even worse. While at uni I'd worked casually in a restaurant where we'd take tinned snails, put them into shells and bury them under butter flavoured with garlic granules. Then we'd freeze the snails and when needed, thaw them in the microwave, grill them, send them out and then wash the shells in the dishwasher when they came back. I'd worked part-time in another place where we had two microwaves going full bore to pump out entrees, and even Con's posh restaurant didn't do much food I was proud of. Especially oysters.

I wanted to get better training. My appetite for good

food was being whetted, thanks to the magazines and newspapers I was reading. I knew there were far better restaurants out there and I wanted to work in one. What I hadn't counted on was going from enthusiastic apprentice to a basket case in health terms within a few months of arriving. I had actually crushed my spine. It was at this time that I met the first private investigator to intrude on my life.

Swanky hotels are considered, or at least were considered then, excellent training grounds, covering all sections of food preparation, and all styles of outlets, from posh restaurants to cafés, from pastry kitchens to butchery.

And the job I landed? A year of phone calls later, one of the better apprentices in my year and crying out for some real training? The job I won as a twenty-six year old who was in it for the passion, the love of cookery?

My fabulous new job was banquet chef three days a week, staff cook two days a week. Banquet sounds grand – but instead of banquet, think function; think bain-marie, and you'll begin to get the picture. In the hierarchy of kitchens, this was pretty close to the bottom. I didn't mind it as a starting point but I was hoping to make the leap to a better outlet soon. As it was, I ended up learning pretty much nothing about international-quality food and a little about mass catering. I also, quite amazingly considering what I'd already seen, learnt far more than before about how crap staff meals could be.

When staff meals fell to me, I'd occasionally get help from a mysterious man I'll call The Shadow; the chef you have when you're not having a chef. I wouldn't call him lazy; after all I'd worked with lazy chefs before and they still managed to do a little bit of work, even if it did seem to happen by accident.

The Shadow's life ambition was to become a firefighter at Canberra airport. Being a smallish city where many firefighters had never been to an actual building fire, at the airport there was a good chance he'd never have to do anything. Anything at all. This bloke was brilliant at becoming invisible for hours on end in a boutique hotel where there was nowhere to hide. He wasn't in the kitchen, he wasn't in the office, he wasn't anywhere to be found. I still think of him when I fly in to Canberra and pray, for more than one reason, that the plane lands safely.

A solo staff cook would start at 8 am and by 11 am was expected to have meals ready to feed up to 140 people with little help and hardly a budget. We did have some bought-in pies and the like and we didn't have to make dessert, because slightly stale sweets – mostly gelatine lumps melting into mirrors from a buffet the night before – appeared like black magic from the pastry kitchen.

For the savoury food you could roast off a few pork necks (delicious), or a curiously tough and unrecognisable cut of beef, but The Shadow's specialty was the soup. It made the German Bastard's Old Boot Soup look like a gourmet's paradise.

The Shadow's only real job was to make sure the banquet coolroom was organised and tidy. So he'd raid the fridge, snaffling everything from leftover, rank-smelling, strangely slimy pastrami that had been sent out twice on a buffet already, to deep-fried potatoes or steamed broccoli, the vegetables left over from a plated meal for 200. He'd fill a large brat pan with the scraps of the kitchen, tossing in other old, fizzy soups and slightly fermented cooked beans and maybe finishing it with smoked salmon. The Shadow would puree it up using a stick blender the size of an outboard motor, and the final result typically looked like the contents of a sewerage outflow pipe. Then it'd be served to staff.

You really don't want to eat the staff meals in most restaurants. Unless you can see the raw ingredients, and trust the chef, most of the dishes are merely scraps that aren't good enough for anyone else. In most restaurants they're cheaply made; and providing them used to mean that waiters could be paid less. So while there may have been Moreton Bay bug tails on the menu, the waiters would be eating fried rice or pasta or consommé scum patties or mould soup, *thanks Chef.*

It was The Shadow who taught me the quickest way to blend up scrambled eggs. 'Just chuck them in,' he'd say, as I cracked eggs, discarding the shell into the bin. 'NO. Not like that, you idiot.'

The Shadow showed me to how to just throw tray after tray of whole eggs into a massive food processor, blitz it, shell and all, and then strain out the finely crushed pale sludge in the bottom. A bit of this sediment, however, usually slipped through. The eggs were cooked in the steamer – as you do with scrambled eggs – and I'm sure they were good for the diners' calcium levels.

At least we used fresh eggs. At another restaurant I made breakfast using a packaged egg product that took forty minutes to scramble, and miraculously – and suspiciously – couldn't be overcooked.

This hotel was supposed to be the world-class training ground I'd been looking for. I didn't expect brilliant food, necessarily, but at least I'd hoped for skills I could use in swank kitchens elsewhere. However, by the time I'd arrived at the hotel the standards had slipped to a pedestrian level. For a start, the pastry kitchen was really just a factory for those gelatine sweets. A $20,000 Italian gelato machine sat idle while even the fanciest restaurant in the building used factory-made ice-cream. All the Danish pastries were bought in, frozen, then baked each morning in the same way I'd done at a pretty ordinary supermarket bakery in my teens.

The expected rotation of apprentices through different sections of the hotel didn't happen. I did get a few hours in the commissary kitchen – a preparation kitchen – where the butcher worked, but he didn't break down whole carcases and do interesting things with meat like I'd heard about. He just rang up other butchers and got them to deliver the meats pre-cut. It was as stimulating as going to the front counter of the butcher down the local shops. I helped a catering section pump out airline meals, seeing how a dollar's worth of ingredients could be made to look like it was worth $10 to the airline. It made the banquet kitchen look smart. Occasionally I'd nick off to pastry to try and learn something, but they'd often just be baking biscuits or using packet pastry, and there were no finer points of technique for a senior apprentice to master by watching and helping with that.

After doing staff meals and banquets for a few months, my constant moans about wanting to do more interesting work hit pay dirt. It was January, the month when a lot of staff wanted a break after the mad December rush. Time to get to the beach; holiday time. So I was offered five days work a week in the hotel's flagship restaurant while one of their chefs went on holiday. It replaced some of my usual shifts, but not all.

Up until that point, I'd been rostered on for weeks at a stretch, and had put in a marathon effort in December. Now at least I was spending about seventy hours a week in the award-winning restaurant. Most swanky hotels in those days had them; the flagship diner that gave the hotel a fabulous, upmarket reputation so you could slop out wedding and conference food from a different kitchen and still charge the earth. This was ours, a place where they charged $22 for a soufflé in the mid-1990s. A place where no matter what hours I worked they filled in my time sheet as forty-two hours a week.

While everybody else took time off, I was still working as hard as ever; stoked to be given a chance to work in the best restaurant at one of the best hotels in town. And just as the opportunity came up, I split my spine.

Following the injury, I was rostered to work every day for another three weeks, still churning out staff meals on my days off from the flagship diner. I didn't want to admit it to myself, but I was suffering every hour of the day. I no longer had the strength to ride my bicycle to work, I no longer ran during my hours off. I was in pain and kept telling my bosses, but they weren't really interested. In the end I had to get a letter from my doctor to get just one day off a week.

The days I did work were still long. Endless twelve-hour shifts began to pile up. I'd spend the time that I wasn't actually working hanging from doorframes in the kitchen to stretch my spine and take the pressure off the discs.

It was a form of traction, where mild relief was followed by wilting pain every time I put weight on my back again.

Work in the poshest restaurant wasn't as exciting as I'd thought. While waiting for the prawns to defrost in the sink, while the food processor pureed avocado with bottled lemon juice (déjà vu from The Hideously Expensive Canberra Restaurant), I'd have my legs swinging and my spine lengthening from a beam or doorframe. Sometimes we'd be allowed a brief meal break, at that same dodgy staff canteen where I cooked on other days.

I spent my free time at the physio. The hotel's executive chef gave me some pointers too. He suggested that maybe it was just like when he had been off for months on stress leave. His doctors had said the problem was all in his mind. He kindly offered up the idea that my pain was imaginary, too, and promptly rejected my one day off a week.

All I wanted to do was cook. I cooked because there was a fire in my belly that was more than hunger, more than ambition, a zealous interest that wouldn't go away. I had swallowed every last bit of pride by returning to the Old German Bastard, tall hat in hand, asking to be trusted and trained again after a falling-out. And then I'd begged for twelve months to get a job at one of the city's leading hotels to receive the best training. I worked inordinately long hours, essentially subsidising the hotel's overseas owners to the tune of thirty hours' overtime a week. I was robbed of my dignity, my rightful income, my right to proper training, and still showed up to work with a broken back pleading for a single day off a week – something most Australians have been taking for granted for the better part of a century. My pain wasn't in my mind.

Life at this time looked pretty bleak. A few days before the accident, in the aftermath of the crazy holiday season, a time when chefs burn themselves down to their cores to make sure the public are fed, I'd argued with my long-term live-in girlfriend. I'd met Lynn at uni, when she was studying nursing. A raven-haired beauty, she knew food better than I did, and she'd been partly responsible for inspiring me to go back to cooking, to follow my dream. When I started work full-time again after uni, we were already renting a flat together.

It's not something to be proud of in an argument, talking to a lover as if they're a kitchenhand, using all the skills you've learnt in the heat of the kitchen. The musician Paul Kelly calls it the 'red mist' that falls before your eyes. A screaming match over nothing is one thing. One that calls up the demons and barbs usually reserved for outbursts in a commercial kitchen, well, that's another thing entirely. Not surprisingly Lynn upped and left our home, moving north, close to family.

By that time, I was off work. For four months after the accident I lived in squalor, unable to wash up without pain. Emptying a washing machine, bending over a sink, sweeping and vacuuming all laid me out for hours afterwards. I couldn't stand, sit or lie for more than a quarter of an hour without feeling wretched from the injury, let alone look after myself. Life fell apart quite quickly.

I felt ashamed of myself for living surrounded by such grime. Eventually a friend came and vacuumed the house. My sixty-three-year-old father washed things for me.

It was, looking on the bright side, as if I'd never be able to do housework again. But in the short term there was no real bright side. I no longer had sensation in parts of my feet and legs. When I could no longer feel the pedals in the car I decided to listen to the doctor. I stopped going to work before there was even more permanent nerve damage. For months, while healing, my diary entries talk of waking in agony at 5.30 am, and the head chef telling me that despite being eligible to finish my apprenticeship, he was refusing to sign the release form. All the while I had no income, and the physio, medical and radiography expenses began to add up.

Management at One of Canberra's Swankiest Hotels chose not to pay me sick leave. I guess $7.70 an hour was too much for them. Because I'd had a work accident, my income had to be paid by worker's compensation – which they also refused. So for the better part of six months I lived off the charity of family. In the end I was left with no option to get my money back (including several thousand dollars in medical bills) than to sue.

The hotel, or perhaps their insurance company, employed a private investigator. She'd followed me, talked to my doctors, my physio, my workmates. After the investigation she met up with me, telling me that she couldn't believe anyone would become a chef, the pay rates were so low.

We settled out of court, against the advice of my solicitor, because I wanted to get on with my life. I didn't want to believe I would always be hurt. Nobody owes me a living and I wanted to get out there and work. And learn. I was still an apprentice, for Christ's sake.

The doctors told me that my injuries would heal as much as they ever would after eighteen months, but that the disc and skeletal damage were permanent. They offered an operation to fuse the vertebrae, with a 5 per cent chance I'd not be able to walk again. One in twenty weren't good enough odds. They told me never to work more than forty hours a week and never lift more than ten kilos. When my back had eventually mended enough to return to work, I tried not to do more than seventy hours on my feet or lift over twenty kilos, but still the job of cooking for a living was always going to be a battle.

For years afterwards I secretly wore a brace that went from above my ribs to below my leg line, a corset-like structure that squeezed the air from my lungs every time I bent over. It made me feel like peeing constantly. Each morning I spent half an hour with my face in the carpet doing exercises to restore some stability to my lower spine. The injury made most work difficult and plagued me in later jobs. I never told prospective employers about it, afraid that they simply wouldn't want someone with a dicky back.

Every day, even now, as I step from bed tiresomely sore, every time I lift a stockpot and wonder if this will cause the next injury to put me out of action for six months, every time I can't do all the things I used to do, from loving to travelling, I'd rather my back was in good nick. Before the injury I'd trekked for months at a stretch, rock climbed, run a marathon and more. A lifelong back injury put an end to most of that.

The injury took me out of work for six months. As soon as I was back at the stove full-time and qualified as a chef, I left the hotel, desperate to try and reignite my career. I took a job in the Blue Mountains with a tightly knit team of three under a renowned chef. After more than a year without working in an à la carte kitchen (the usual madhouse kitchen, where the food is cooked and plated to order from a menu, as opposed to functions that have a set menu), and an imposed six months lay-off, my skills were rusty. Squashed into my brace, with hands softened by months out of work, I didn't do a great job.

The restaurant had many good things going for it, not least some of the finest produce I'd ever seen or even imagined. We received freshwater fish within hours of it being killed, cooked excellent game birds, picked wild mushrooms and used the rarest wild strawberries. But thanks to some quite awful accommodation it didn't really work out. For two weeks I bunked down in the local youth hostel, constantly being woken by drunks. Later, in a private hotel that another chef dubbed the 'home for homeless men,' I woke to find blood soaking the tiles in the shower. At another house, living with five waitresses and a chef from the restaurant, I'd get up in the middle of the night to discover evidence of a serious assault in the kitchen and maggots in the bin.

Meanwhile, the big smoke, Sydney, now only ninety minutes away, started to exert its gravitational pull, not least because Lynn was living there. We began dining at the best restaurants on my days off, me driving back from town early in the morning to work, often reeking of Darley Street Thai or Merrony's or excellent Cantonese. Within months, I bailed out of the Blue Mountains, betraying the trust of the chef who hired me, and flung myself into the madhouse of the city, and into the arms of a woman who'd already left me once.

*

I thought city restaurants could be insane, although I never believed they could be as crazy as they were. But I've no-one else to blame. Here I was, in the country's largest city. Sydney's food scene was expanding rapidly, with world-class chefs and design-driven restaurants that would define an era. I was half broken, my skills stale, but also driven to get into one of Sydney's finest.

I should've spent time strengthening my spine at a modest job, re-learning the finer points of service (you lose the touch after just a few days off the pans), but I felt I'd lost too much time already. I was impatient to learn. I had discovered that there was an immense gulf between good food and bad, and unlike some people I could taste the difference. I desperately wanted to work in a restaurant that cooked the kind of food that I wanted to eat.

To get a job in the right place, or even the wrong place, wasn't easy, despite the fact that restaurants were desperate for chefs. I worked fourteen hours at one restaurant as a pay-free 'trial' only to be told at the end of the shift that they'd given the job away the week before. At another, where I cracked my head on a low doorway and just about laid myself out cold, I was apparently 'overqualified'. And the restaurant I did land a job in? While it represented everything I believed about top-tier cooking – chopping onions just prior to service, baking bread twice a day, soups put through a hand-turned mill rather than the ubiquitous food processor, everything made from scratch – this restaurant had more sinister problems.

I'd been warned about the owners. Repeatedly. And I should've realised that having worked one day for free, then being asked to come back for a second free day, that I wasn't going to be showered with rewards. In fact, I was never actually told I had got the job, just that I was on trial for a week, then on trial for a second week, and then a third. Admittedly, I did get paid after the first two days. But there I saw, first hand, the truly malevolent side of restaurants.

Food, while it may be a big thing in the press, while it may make some people lots of money, while I've earned my income from it, raved on about it for thousands of words and bored people rigid with my views and reviews, food is just sewage the next day. Yes, it is a privilege to have enough to eat, and it's good to eat well. Food can make lots of people happy for many reasons, but in the whole scheme of life, restaurant food is not that important.

I realised I was in the wrong place when I saw the owner of this restaurant tell off a Chinese kitchenhand. The kitchenhand had rung to say he couldn't come in that night because he was a student working illegally and a triad were threatening to dob him in. The owner was screaming obscenities down the telephone, ranting and belittling him.

By the time the police had left the next day, the chef was in tears. Apparently that same kitchenhand had jumped, or perhaps been pushed, underneath a train at a city station, and the only identifying paper on him was a payslip from the restaurant. I felt sick. Forget the handmade noodles, the clever spicing, the signature potatoes. That was a pretty obscene way to treat a human being. His death left a dark stain on all our minds.

Of course I left. But not on good terms. I gave notice, but they refused to advertise my job and expected me to work longer after I'd resigned than I had before. I was working up to fourteen hours a day and yet was accused of abusing their good nature.

'You fucking used us,' the restaurant's co-owner screamed, as though I'd planned on quitting before I'd even arrived. 'How dare you leave us before we've filled your job,' she yelled. In an horrific screaming match (and I don't scream) at the front of the restaurant, they threatened me, abused me and told me I was a fucking lazy prick anyway. I wasn't their finest chef, that's for sure, still with rusty skills and a broken back. I also had plenty to learn to become as efficient as others in their marvellous, committed brigade. But I had also seen the red of their eyes close up and I'd had enough of their good nature. It's just food. It isn't worth selling your soul over.

Post-screaming match, I still had little money in the bank. I needed my last pay cheque so I went back to work after a two-day break and vanished for good on pay night. It was a few days earlier than I had told them I'd be finishing. On the way home from work that last night, an apprentice from the restaurant noticed I'd taken my toolbox with me.

'You're not coming back, are you?' he said gleefully.

I felt terrible. I have always tried to do the honourable thing and there I was sneaking out of a restaurant that expected me back at work the next day. I was letting down a whole team, people already on the edge of exhaustion, chefs whose passion and commitment makes most professions look lame. I'd become the kind of chef that had pained me as an apprentice, one that lacked dignity and responsibility.

'No,' I answered, apologetically, 'I can't put up with that kind of shit.' I asked him to tell the others in the kitchen – but not the boss – that I meant them no harm, but that I wouldn't stick around to see people treated with contempt. He laughed, said it was the best thing that I could do, and that everybody would be saying good on me for shoving it up the owners of the restaurant.

The apprentices, he told me, were so exhausted that they used their TAFE days to sleep rather than go to college, the only way they could make it through the weeks.

The next morning, at precisely the hour I was due to start work, I was outside the bank waiting for it to open so I could cash my final cheque. I was disheartened and poor, and that money had to get me through more than one week.

To pay the rent I took another job through an agency. In that hotel kitchen I watched as one chef completely lost it.

'Shut the fuck up, bitch,' I arrived in the kitchen to hear him say to the night chef. Then he threatened to visit her home and rape her. It was vile, frightening behaviour, an expression of anger at its most raw. When human resources heard about it, I was called in as a witness.

'We believe,' the HR manager said without meeting my eye, 'that there's been swearing in the kitchen.'

Fuck me dead, swearing in a kitchen?

That's when I realised that people who don't know kitchens just don't get it. I'd seen a woman being threatened with violent sexual assault by some gangster in a chef's hat and all HR worry about are a few reprobates swearing? They must be kidding if they think they can manage kitchens when they don't recognise the type of people, and the type of attitude, that pervades the industry. At least they did the right thing in one respect, as the bloke concerned never worked another shift.

It wasn't just Sydney's jobs that gave me quivers.

Blame it on coffee, if you like, but heart palpitations had become part of my big-city reality. I had suddenly discovered properly made coffee, stuff that wasn't as bitter as an old chef. I was working long hours, so any time I was offered a brew I'd take it to pep myself up. I went from zero cups to about twelve cups a day in a couple of weeks. From someone who'd just nick the chocolate off someone else's cappuccino, I turned into someone flying on caffeine. On the way to work I'd break into a sweat, my heart pounding so strongly that my body shook and my hands trembled. I thought the breathless, nervous state was just another part of city stress.

Life was spiralling out of control. Soon after I walked out on the first crazy restaurant, Lynn left. Again. I was wired but despondent, angry and feeling let down by my employers. Living in a tiny bedsit, sleeping on the floor, with a $15 cane couch as the only furniture, counting coins to be able to buy food, times were tough. As a breakfast chef I cooked at home every night, surviving on brown rice and lentils and a large spice collection for months. The view out the window was of the wife basher on the fourth floor of the flat opposite, my social life non-existent.

In the days after Lynn left I consoled myself with a bottle of chardonnay and a nugget of Kervella's marvellous ashed goat's cheese. It cost more than $100 a kilogram, and it was worth every cent. Each mouthful was a revelation, a complex, fascinating flavour that affected my mood, lifting my spirits. It cheered me up in a way I'd never known food could. In a block of virginal white cheese I'd found a mini salvation, and a reinforcement of what I had come to suspect: no matter what life threw at me, I was going to be affected in an extraordinary way by tucker.

At this time, with no friends in Sydney and a heart-breakingly empty and loveless flat, I toyed with the idea of writing articles for the paper. Not for the money, but for the distraction, the outlet, and to learn about food in a way that no restaurant seemed capable of teaching me. I wanted to share this emotional pleasure I seemed to get from food.

My back injury had forced me into countless practitioners' waiting rooms where I'd been immersed in the food sections of magazines. Most had recipes and a blurb of some kind. In my fervour to be involved with food I'd spend idle time reading about it. Being shadowed by back pain gave me the chance to become interested in cooking from a voyeuristic standpoint, the journalistic and readers' standpoint. I was amazed and inspired by passionate writing and felt personally betrayed by formulaic or erroneous stories. Recipes could be either predictable or exciting, depending on where you looked, and the stories ranged from dull (the majority) to extraordinary. There certainly wasn't the broad range of food magazines you'll find today, but I did find inspiration in *Vogue Entertaining* and *Gourmet Traveller*, and adored the look and feel of *Country Style*.

Without knowing it then, throughout that bleak time, I was honing skills, learning the art of food writing that would one day earn me a living. But before that happened I had a couple more years filled with the wonder of professional cooking, in three states, including finally making and selling food I loved.

I was soon to start a new job, in the town where I grew up, and for the first time in my career I was going to be asked my opinion. It was pretty daunting, but pretty bloody exciting, too.

7

Chef's hat

MOVING BACK to Canberra was really my only option, scary as that may sound to those who've never lived there.

I'd run out of money. I'd hated my jobs. I couldn't afford to run a car. In Canberra I had a place to live, some family who cared, and things were improving, food-wise. I knew there were now at least three restaurants where the food was good.

I picked one out, rang them, went in and got a job. There were four qualified chefs working at The Republic when I arrived, plus a couple of apprentices. It was a modern, buoyant kitchen, the hours were pretty good, and I could sit back and relax for most of my fifty hours a week. I was just another face in the kitchen; all care, no responsibility. The produce was first rate, the restaurant smart, the food cooked well and the service switched on – ideal, really.

Problem was, the owners were losing money. Within a fortnight of starting they asked me why they were spending $1000 a week more than they should on food. The answer was staring them in the face. It's a lesson for all owners of restaurants, if you don't know or understand the kitchen, you won't be able to control it. In the end, chefs will stiff you every time.

I already knew what was going wrong, at least in part, just by having my eyes open. To prove it, for a week I recorded what hit the garbage bin. 'This smells like my arse,' I'd say, using an expression I'd learnt from Fritz as whole beef fillets, the most expensive cut of meat, went slimy and had to be thrown away. Hundreds of dollars of seafood went off. Vegetables festered, salad yellowed and composted in bags, soups fizzled; pretty much the whole inventory went off at some point. It wasn't bad cooking – thank the lord that I'd left that behind – and it wasn't an abuse of privilege. It was just poor management and organisation.

To be fair, the staff who headed up the kitchen, two co-head chefs, had been promoted after the original high-profile cook had left and they probably weren't up to the task. Suddenly, however, I was being offered the head chef's role in a kitchen where I was the last person in the door. Part of me said no, that I didn't have the skills to run a kitchen, or the back strength, or the repertoire. My confidence had been undermined and I doubted I was up to the task, either.

Nobody had ever asked my opinion on a menu before. Input was discouraged at most places I'd worked, and here I was, being offered the job of writing whole menus, ordering all the food, deciding how things should be cooked and by whom. It was a chance to shine or fail. Within a month I went from someone who just shut his mouth and worked, to someone with a voice.

It was by far the most exciting time in my career, and the scariest – no-one else to blame, no-one else to shoulder the responsibility. I'd wake in the middle of the night with dishes, flavours and textures rolling around in my head. Inspiration came from a daily walk to the fruit market across town, or from the producers I'd visit, or who arrived at the door. I'd drive three hours to check out goat's cheese and pick up a good supply. I'd ring fish farmers to ask about colour variation, sourdough bread producers to see what they made that I might be able to use, apple growers, oyster farmers and top-end Sydney suppliers.

Surprisingly, I seemed blessed with the capacity to put flavours together in my head. I had plenty more ideas than time – most not from restaurants I'd worked in, rather from cookbooks I'd read – and it was a godsend to have an ability to taste combinations before they hit the plate. And while I did push the envelope, treading on some pretty shaky territory with the cooking, more than 90 per cent of the dishes that I hoped might work ended up as winners on the menu. Of the other 10 per cent, some were out-and-out failures that didn't last long. Others didn't make it past the first trial cook-up.

It was at this restaurant that I learnt the true joy of professional cooking. Up until then, cooking had often been marred by bad ingredients. Thanks to the subnormal personalities I'd had to cope with in kitchens, the work had been more a case of enduring than thriving. The staff were either culinary or genuine criminals. But at The Republic I loved arriving in the kitchen early in the morning and going through the coolroom, chatting to suppliers, prodding them to get the best produce, whinge-ing, cajoling, praising and supporting. The team I gathered were excellent, though we did have our moments getting the brigade together.

At one stage I had a second chef who didn't always come to work when supposed to. Always a bit late, always a bit lazy, she'd take phone calls in the middle of service and let the rest of the team take up the slack. When she didn't arrive at work on the busiest lunch of the year, and I found her actually sitting in the restaurant, drunk, having let the whole team down all week, I sacked her. I'd like to blame it on the kind of management training I'd had, but I probably would've sacked her anyway. It was December 23. My family called me Scrooge that Christmas.

I went for months without a second chef, and so that additional role fell to me. At one stage I took on a cook with whom I'd worked at One of Canberra's Swankiest Hotels. He was older than me, but he was pretty crap at his job, not knowing the rice for risotto was different than the one you'd use for pilaf and that the two weren't interchangeable. With ten years more experience than me, his lack of passion and knowledge seemed staggering. His palate was that of someone in their teens, rather than someone with over a decade of professional cooking. His knives were blunt, his skills rudimentary. My only regret, apart from hiring him, is that he resigned before I had a chance to throw him out.

I don't know if I was a good manager. After all, the management style I'd been taught hadn't been very friendly or insightful. I did rant and rave. I did bellow at the apprentices when they didn't seem to be listening. I did sack three people on the spot for incompetence or refusal to do their work. And I did pay a huge price for having standards about who to hire and who to let go, working many more long, hard, stressful hours in a short-staffed kitchen thanks only to myself. The thing is, a kitchen has to have rules, people have to do things at a certain time, in a certain way, or the food ends up burnt, cold, raw, late or just plain horrible.

While trying to enforce a structure and a hierarchy, I fought hard trying not to become the spiteful, vindictive, mean and nasty person who I'd despised when I was training. God knows if I succeeded or not, though one apprentice that I used to rouse on endlessly invited me to his wedding in 2006. Another rushed up to me at a local market years after we'd worked together, not with a cleaver, but to chat. So at least if I was a tyrant they didn't harbour grudges.

Eventually, I promoted a former apprentice to the second chef's job. What a dream it was. He didn't try to change things every time my back was turned, he worked hard and I like to think we treated him well, from his pay packet to his shifts. His touch on the dishes I'd created left me inspired, and there was a sense of relief knowing I could take a day off without the whole menu going to the dogs. At the same time I had an apprentice who seemed able to read my mind, taking a new dish and plating it with flair and precision, creating a better meal than I'd had in my head or created with my hands. Together we served some incredible dishes for the prices we charged, all prepared from pristine ingredients.

By the time the kitchen had settled down, I had a brilliant team. We had a lovely modern restaurant. The owners trusted me with their asset and I tried my hardest to make food that we could all be proud of. We'd braise fresh ducks for curries, the curry paste pounded and pureed from scratch. We'd roll our own black pepper noodles. We made sensational brandade, a potato and salt cod puree that tasted much better than it sounds. We dished up a stunning herb-scented lamb, along with some succulent beetroot-marinated kangaroo on a silken white bean puree. We also made things I had no idea about. My tarte tatin was a barely passable rendition of a dish I'd never eaten, only read about. The chicken confit with pumpkin and pappardelle (wide ribbon pasta) was always a work in progress. But most of the dishes, most of the time, were actually pretty decent.

Not that everything ran smoothly. I'd put a dish on the menu, teach the team how to cook it, watch them, help them, supervise them as they prepared it for six weeks, then turn around once to find they'd changed the whole thing. I learnt that every dish, no matter what it is, will bear the seal of the hand that cooked it. The same recipe reacts differently to a different cook, each individual adding their own subtleties, each weaving nuances through the process of cooking, resting, spicing and plating. Food that doesn't bear the stamp of the hand that cooks it becomes soulless and austere. Not bad, just lacking passion; formulaic food that one day I'd spend way too much time reviewing. My food wasn't the same when one of my chefs cooked it, in the same way that a singer adds their own nuances to someone else's song. Surprisingly, and thankfully, not all the changes they wrought were bad.

It was at this restaurant that I had first-hand contact with restaurant critics. While I'd worked before at restaurants that had been reviewed, now *I* was being reviewed; it was MY food, MY menu, MY team. A local paper seemed enamoured of us, coming in for a freebie, getting pissed and giving us a good write-up. *The Canberra Times* loved us, reviewers praised us, and we had a pretty discerning audience that kept coming back. But the most interesting thing was being visited by *The Sydney Morning Herald*'s restaurant critic, Terry Durack. I'd met him a few months before when I challenged him at a function about a review he'd written, and should've spotted him from the open kitchen, his distinctive mop of dark hair and regulation black skivvy a dead giveaway. The waiters had seen him taking notes at the table, but nobody suspected he was a reviewer or pointed him out until he poked his head in the kitchen after dinner. An open kitchen isn't somewhere you spend all your time looking out during service, though I kind of wish I had. Maybe it's better I didn't, because I treated him like Just Another Dickhett. Not that it was the ideal time to be reviewed. It was the second day of a new menu, we were up to our eyeballs in new dishes, we had a full house, we were running out of food, and generally in the shit. At least I was cooking, so there was no-one else to blame.

Durack ordered dishes I was most proud of – brandade, kangaroo, the crème caramel. But he also ordered a train crash; the dish on the menu that I didn't know how to cook. In my head it was glass noodles – a delicate salad of translucent Asian mung bean noodles, flavoured gently with herbs and fragrant coconut milk, with a few perfect seared sea scallops dotted through. In reality, because I didn't know how to cook glass noodles, it was a snotty, flat, badly textured mess of a dish. The flavours were good, the idea was probably okay, but the execution was pathetic.

I was mortified that we'd sent this mangled dish out to anyone before it was perfected, but particularly to a reviewer – it makes the humiliation so much more public. The glass noodle dish was off the menu the next day. When Durack rang the following week to talk about the meal, I told him how shamed I felt that he'd ordered it. And Durack, to his credit, never mentioned it again. Not in print, not in restaurant guides, nowhere. It was eye opening to see that my remorse and embarrassment wouldn't be multiplied by a public haranguing. He didn't love everything about the restaurant or my food, but what he liked he gave a good rap. And the one train crash of a dish that appeared on a new menu for barely a day was forgotten.

I learnt a lot from that. I learnt that humility wasn't a bad thing, that telling someone you didn't think the dish worked was better than trying to bluff your way through. It was a lesson I took with me into a life of reviewing. I learnt it was all too easy to find fault, but more important to promote those looking to improve.

In that year as head chef I learnt about *The Sydney Morning Herald Good Food Guide*, its cachet and its power. In the 1996 edition The Republic earnt a chef's hat, the local equivalent of a Michelin star, though with very different criteria. Only three NSW restaurants had the highest award, three chef's hats, and only one other Canberra restaurant was good enough to get a single hat: a sign of consistently good food with a touch of magic. Unexpected and yet greatly appreciated, our hat was recognition of the hard work the owners, waiters and chefs had put in. Judged by Durack as co-editor of the *Guide*, it was the ultimate approval of what we had tried to do as a team. By the time we travelled to

Sydney for the big awards ceremony piss-up, however, I already had my sights set further afield.

Canberra had been good to me, but I still felt a need to be doing better things. My Thai-style deep-fried whole snapper, an ugly but sensational dish, was banned by one of the restaurant's owners because it didn't look pretty. Local diners didn't understand that you could serve a spinach salad, thinking spinach had to be cooked. I was pushed down on food costs, and irritated when a quiet week was followed by insecurity and changes in the business plan, when sometimes a quiet week is part of the annual cycle. At one stage I contemplated buying the restaurant, but it was too expensive, the rent too high, the fitout too smart for me to pay off as a loan.

While the work was going exceptionally well, Sydney's world-class dining scene still had a hold on me. I still, stupidly, fancied Lynn, and we were back sharing meal-times. (With apologies to Billy Bragg, I used to think love was blind, but now I realise it's just a bit short-sighted.) Predictably, then, I spent a lot of days fleeing Canberra to dine in Sydney's better restaurants. The produce was more varied, the atmosphere sexier, the mood so much more upbeat. It was thrilling to see dishes raved over by diners, to find restaurants abuzz with foodies, talking, drinking, laughing and comparing notes on the best places to eat.

In Canberra I could eat brilliant seafood at Ottoman Cuisine, and dine moderately well at a few other places, but in Sydney there was so much more going on. I trawled Chinatown and Cabramatta. I went to Leichhardt, so-called Little Italy (and wondered why it was so dire). I spent my money at innumerable stunning bistros, contemporary Australian, Chinese, Italian and modern Greek restaurants. There was so much excitement in the hospitality industry, so many food-savvy customers and such food-savvy media that I was gagging to be a part of it. My plan was to revisit Australia's culinary capital and try to establish myself as head chef in a kitchen of note.

I gave the restaurant three months' notice. Leading up to the move, everything was in order. I vacated the flat I rented. Then Lynn vanished with no forwarding details. And then my car gave up and died.

In one week I left my job, lost my car, my place to live and finally farewelled my girlfriend of six years. Luckily I still had most of my spine.

8

Not a good way to make a living

A HEAD CHEF ROLE in Sydney never eventuated, but by the time I'd left Canberra for the last time I already had another outlet for my passions: writing occasional pieces for the food section of *The Canberra Times*. However, freelance writing certainly wasn't paying the bills. My reasonably high profile as a local chef had allowed me to get some things published, but when they paid me, if they paid me, it was often a nominal sum.

Becoming a freelance writer taught me many things. It taught me that 'freelance' is another word for poor. It taught me that rejection is a constant companion. And I despise rejection. I was lucky; the first piece I sent away was accepted. When almost all of the next ten were rejected, it hurt, but I don't think I would've kept writing if the first few stories I'd written had landed in the bin.

My first article for *The Australian* was a piece on British food writer and one-time TV chef Fanny Cradock. She was my hero, a woman who ranted about 'tearing strips off your greengrocer' if they didn't let you squeeze the fruit, and quipped that the only place to toss a crepe that was thick enough to toss was in the bin. The story was picked up by *The Australian*'s 'Time and Tide' editor, whatever that section was. They didn't seem to have a dedicated food section. Fanny had, apparently, passed away months previously, though I didn't know it, and the editor thought my piece would make a nice obituary. *The Australian* paid me a pretty substantial amount compared to my normal wage, far more than the local press, too. I rang 'Time and Tide' and said I had written other stories they may be interested in. The editor sounded doubtful. Sure enough, he wasn't interested in stories on eggs or hazelnuts, cheese or trout.

Not that I was going to let that stop me. I wrote plenty of articles, even sent some of them away to see if they could be published. With no permanent home and some time to kill, I hung around on the NSW south coast for a month, thinking about the future, writing pieces, cooking at home every night, wondering what should be my next move. It was to be back to Sydney but in what capacity was still undecided. I'd been cooking so well, in such a good environment, I was loath to step back into someone else's kitchen. I needed and wanted to learn, but wasn't willing to compromise standards to do it. There was another thing: my back.

At The Republic I'd held myself together well enough. My team didn't tell the boss when I disappeared for twenty minutes at a time to prostrate myself on a hard floor when the pain came. I knew I could work reasonably long hours and cope, but not if I couldn't control the work. And writing seemed to be a good fallback for someone whose years at the stove were always going to be a challenge.

I still find it easier to cook dinner than construct a thousand words to keep a reader interested, but to begin with my writing was extraordinarily dull. I'd mimic the style of articles in reference books, thinking that was the right thing to do, but despairing that I wasn't able to convey the joy of eating. Gradually I threw off the explanatory style, attempting to make the words embody more of eating's pleasures, sensually and emotionally. Oh, and I always tried to make them fit the eighth column of the newspaper, the one that editors always needed some copy, any copy, to fill.

As I wrote, I tried different techniques to garner attention. The important thing then, as now, wasn't that someone cooks my recipes, or believes my views, but that they get excited about food through something I've said or described: through my words.

After a year in Canberra and a few weeks of hanging out on the south coast enjoying my time off, I moved back to Sydney and worked teaching trainee cooks.

All this time, from my first stint in Sydney working as a chef, writing on time off, I dined out when I could: the training job was daytime hours, so nights were mine. For years I ate out several times a week.

Eating at a great restaurant became my adrenaline rush. It was my bungee jump, my tandem skydive. I cooked for a living, went to restaurants for fun, and rejoiced at any opportunity to dine out. My skin prickled with the anticipation; the sounds, sights, smells of a good restaurant thrilled me to my core. Restaurant dining made me inordinately happy. They say a good meal, like good wine, a good run and good sex, releases endorphins, the natural high. Maybe I had switched addictions after the accident, from exercise to eating, from running to sitting, from wide-open spaces to the rarefied atmosphere of deliriously good diners.

Since my teens I'd been the kind of sick puppy who was happy dining alone in places that throbbed with hospitality. I found that the pulse of a good restaurant was clearly audible if you were listening. Dining with others is a pleasure, but a truly extraordinary restaurant can, in some ways, become diluted by company. In bad places having someone to eat with made the restaurant a whole lot more enjoyable. But I never had money enough to pay for anyone else anyway. I budgeted on going, alone, to at least one new café, a new bistro and new restaurant every week, as well as established eateries when the money allowed.

I was still cooking for a living, doing mostly anonymous and quite ghastly jobs. But then I picked up a part-time reviewing gig with the same *Good Food Guide* in which I'd recently won a hat. Ironically, although I was now based in Sydney, my job was to review Canberra restaurants, and so I spent that year, and the next three, when I lived in Melbourne, travelling back to the city of my childhood and visiting restaurants I was intimately familiar with. It was a proviso that I couldn't work in a restaurant – even in another city – while I was a reviewer. Training work, nursing homes, function and boardroom work was fine, but not restaurants. Ethics became a strong part of my reviewing philosophy from the start.

By this stage I was already addicted to dining out. Sure, the $20 payment per restaurant was so low as to be laughable, not coming close to covering the cost of travel, and the budget per place not enough to cover the cost of all the food. But my dining companions kicked in for BYO alcohol, ate what I told them and provided excellent company. We chomped our way across Canberra and surrounds that year, and the next and the next, eating at around thirty restaurants I'd sussed out in order to find sixteen or twenty worth covering for the *Guide*.

What started out as a job covering one region rapidly spread to be many regions and three cities a year later. I asked everywhere for recommendations, rang high commissions, expats, food-savvy locals, checked out other guides and talked to chefs. I learnt not to trust tourist offices or taxidrivers — but found that wine makers and food store owners often had the good oil. I also took the occasional punt based on a look in the window and a read of the menu, virtually always to no avail. A recommendation is a very good thing.

In my first job after The Republic, I worked full-time for a year, training cooks for a private company in Sydney. Imagine Jamie Oliver's Fifteen without the financial backing, the high profile or the vetting of 2000 applicants. It was just like on telly, though these students often had zero motivation, more attitude, and, unlike Jamie, we couldn't afford to lose £2 million on it in two years. We didn't even have a permanent kitchen or a budget to buy much of the food the curriculum demanded. It was a privately run training scheme designed to scam the government by short-changing the trainees. I was hardly qualified to be dealing with the students, either.

The trainees would be kicked off the dole if they didn't attend a course, so their enthusiasm was non-existent. Some had come from overseas, where servants did the cooking and cleaning, and didn't take kindly to instruction. Some were just ratbags who were always a hair's breadth away from trouble with the law (rather like a lot of cooks I knew, actually). And a few were vaguely interested in what actually happens in a kitchen.

As trainers we had to show them everything from sharpening knives to hand-stretched filo pastry, according to the curriculum. The regime was old-fashioned cooking – white sauce, dressed crab, curry cooked with banana and sultanas, just as I'd been taught. In contrast to the industry they were training for, and my training, the ability to cook a dish once would get the student a pass, though many couldn't repeat their success even a single day later.

One group of trainees was completely different. This was a mob of Aboriginal students who had chosen to learn about cooking. A woman younger than my mother sobbed when I asked what sort of bush tucker she might know about – the eating of it was banned in the missions where she grew up; these people had been flogged for speaking their own tongue. In our first week we did a walking tour around hotel foyers in Sydney, only to find security following us everywhere. I'd taken two previous groups of students to these hotels, but the only hotel that dealt with an Aboriginal group the same way as a white group was the Observatory, giving us an unprompted, unsolicited private tour on the spur of the moment.

Teaching, especially teaching a disadvantaged minority, was the hardest job I've ever done. One student was homeless before he came to us, needing life skills more than knife skills. He occasionally went missing for several days at a time, returning to class still wearing the same uniform he had disappeared in, unwashed and slept-in since he last attended class. I learnt that if you wanted a dry, safe place to sleep you should catch the eleven pm train over the Blue Mountains to Lithgow and back each night. I learnt that gambling is the enemy of some souls, two of whom vanished from the class for up to a week following each payday.

Success was measured differently with this group. You didn't care if they couldn't make a velouté or bone out a sole, you were just happy if they got their life in order.

I was told by one woman, after four months of full-time training, that she hated men. *Really* hated men. What's more, she really, really hated white men. Her brother had taken 'a lift to the shops' forty years previously with the white mission manager. He was adopted out with no word given to his family for decades; one of Australia's shameful Stolen Generations. Anyway, she told me that she hated white men with a vengeance, but that for some reason she liked me. I still have a poem she wrote about how they used to surreptitiously speak their own language at the mission.

Another woman told me that no matter how far away I got, I would always be invading her personal space and that she didn't hate all men, just me. Every single student had harrowing personal backgrounds, their stories heartbreaking, and their basic home-cooking skills barely existent.

My students tried me, tested me, pained me. It's hard to stay confident when all ten students don't show up for class one day. But they taught me a lot about the value of relationships, the shallowness of hospitality (try being refused service because of your companion's race, for a start). One of them, the man who had been homeless before the six-month course started, won a scholarship to a hotel cooking school. I stumbled across a former student years later in a city street, finding that he was still in chef's whites long after I'd left the trade. Another, a brickies' labourer, used to bring me cheesecake that he'd learnt to cook, and had become famed for in his neighbourhood. He never did leave the building industry, but he thankfully learnt a few things to cook at home. Yet another student I saw staggering around Sydney's Central Station sporting a puffy, scarred face and blackened eye, a man behind her threatening me with his fists when I tried to say g'day.

While teaching taught me some things about life, it also sucked me down to my very marrow. I staggered out of the job drained and exhausted, not an eighty-hour-week, frypan-throwing exhausted, rather an emotionally spent exhausted. Teachers must be made of very good stuff.

During the year of teaching, I was writing more regularly, and for the first time actually being paid for each piece that was published. I'd sent in a story idea to *Gourmet Traveller* magazine and had it accepted, my first to hit a national mag. *Vogue Entertaining* also wanted me to write for them after I sent them a similar piece. It was tempting to think that if I wrote often enough, and interestingly enough, it might be possible to make a living at this game, or at least lead an interesting life trying.

Foodie fervour gripped me so badly it hurt. I felt a longing for a certain, specific type of job that wasn't cooking. I wanted to review restaurants. I wanted to be in these magical places, eating food that was better than could be imagined, with flavours I'd never conceived of. I wanted to absorb the electricity that a full dining room generates, to sit amidst skilful staff, knowledgeable wine waiters and be cooked for by incredibly talented chefs.

In short, I wanted someone else's job. I didn't know whose, but somebody's. Professional restaurant reviewers are thin on the ground. You don't see the job advertised in the paper. When I was training as a chef I didn't even know such a job existed. Back then it probably didn't, not as a profession. I desperately wanted to hang around restaurants. So, after a year in Sydney, I decided to move to Melbourne. I figured if you want to be a restaurant reviewer, you should first understand cafés, and if any Australian city understands cafés, it's Melbourne. Rated by many as the best coffee outside Rio and Seattle, not to mention the whole of Italy, Melbourne's café society rocked. It still does.

Melbourne is to Sydney what Naples is to Milan. Its top-end restaurants may not be quite as design savvy, it may not be as international, or as expensive, or as up itself, but it does most things better, most of the time, and cafés it does brilliantly well.

So, on a glimmer of hope, but without the promise of regular (or any) work, I left Sydney again.

I decided that the only credible restaurant reviewer is a highly experienced eater – and one who eats everything. I felt partially qualified, but for me, eating everything was no mean feat. I'd been a virtual vegetarian a few years before this. Although I was at a point where I'd taste any food for work, eating a full meal of steak or other heavy meats meant a shift in my mindset and my constitution.

But if you want to be a public palate, you have to eat things. While I had no interest in devouring endangered species, anything else was fair, ahem, game.

At this point I had learnt to taste dishes, appreciate their character, and recognise their flaws, and separate that from a personal bias. I could rave about a dish I didn't actually want to eat myself. I could see the value in meals that, if I wasn't a reviewer, I wouldn't be ordering. I would eat anything, apart from kidneys, which I find incredibly hard to swallow, and squid ink, which for a time used to make my throat swell up (pass the pocket knife and a biro for the home tracheotomy, please). In short, apart from a few biases, I felt ready. But first I needed to get a bit more experience under my belt.

I treated myself to a month gorging in France, everywhere from the bistro where you get zero choice to three Michelin star restaurants, the crème de la crème of France's cooking. I went to Troisgros, Lucas Carton, L'Arpège, Georges Blanc and more. I dined at lunchtime to save money, making a half bottle of the second cheapest wine last through the savoury part of the ten or twelve courses. I stayed in youth hostels, often in towns a long way from the restaurants in question. I bought a jacket and tie to try and look the part, only to find the French in summer holiday mode and open-necked shirts. Clutching the *Guide Rouge*, the red-bound Michelin guide to French restaurants, I looked like an elder from the Church of Latter Day Saints more than a taste junkie. In four weeks I spent just about all the money I had on a trip that altered the way I looked at food forever.

Immediately prior to leaving and on my return I also

ate at Australia's best. I was awestruck by the slow-cooked duck at Rockpool, surprised but a little let down by Paul Bocuse, seriously blown away at Claude's, mesmerised by Jacques Reymond. And I travelled to them all on public transport or by shank's pony. At least I always arrived hungry.

By the time I arrived in Melbourne I'd been touched by greatness, the best chefs in France, the UK and Australia. Yet I had no regular income, no job to go to, no friends who'd put me up for more than a week, and no idea what I was doing. Luckily being a chef means you can pick up work anywhere. I joined an agency and waited for the six o'clock phone calls each morning to fill in for other chefs. I helped with functions, worked boardrooms, churned out meals at the MCG, but mostly it was staff cafeteria kind of work – all at the kind of places that would never be reviewed.

In this environment I learnt that you never stop learning. What were curried sausages? How do you cook pasta that will sit in a bain-marie for hours and not go soggy (answer: you can't). Most of it was half-processed food slopped out for the employees of money-conscious corporations. Interestingly, however, some big company boardrooms and law firms have food that makes hatted restaurant food look dodgy.

I moved to Melbourne with nothing more than a banana box full of office equipment and a backpack. Unlike most restaurant reviewers I knew, I was self funded but poor. Restaurant critics come from many backgrounds, but when I started reviewing, the dominant industry that spawned reviewers was advertising. In the 1980s and

1990s advertising types ate out. They had a high disposable income, plus an expense account, and they were the kind of people who were happy to spend it on lunch. Advertising people are good with words (well, some are), good with ideas and good at making a point. In contrast, I was a normal person with an abnormal obsession and a below normal income. I did have first-hand experience of restaurants, though, and if I had money to spend, that's where I spent it.

The harder I worked, the luckier I became. The editor of *The Age*'s food section, 'Epicure', explained that whoever spotted a new café could review it for her. So day and night I scoured the streets by tram, on foot, by pushbike. I didn't know what had been in the paper in the months prior to arriving in our Paris of the south, but I was pretty sure I could tell the age of a café by looking at how clean the windows were, how scuffed the walls and chairs were, and the quality of the fixtures and fittings. A new café was a café gagging to be reviewed. Despite the fact that Melbourne cafés were in a retro mood – all 1960s laminate tables and reclaimed kitchen chairs – within a few weeks, and despite the competitiveness of others who also wanted to write about cafés, I had my first review in the paper.

Shortly afterwards I picked up my first regular gig writing about cafés for *The Age*, probably because I knew more about what was opening than just about anybody. It helps if you don't have a normal job. While reviewing is competitive in theory, few people could spare the time I did simply looking for a good brew. Days spent pedalling the bike through Melbourne's streets were starting to pay off. I earned $150 some weeks, $75 on others, depending on the place and length of story. And for the first time my rent was covered by my writing. But only my rent.

It was at this time that I learnt how to spot a good café before I'd even sat down. You have to if you're going to be an efficient reviewer. A good café usually has a few people drinking coffee in it. I'd check the insides of their empty cups – properly foamed milk leaves a thick smudge down the side whereas overheated or badly treated milk doesn't. I'd check the sweets – congealing custards and stale, curling pastries meant a bad café – and if the cakes were more than about ten centimetres tall, they were typically not worth ordering: they seemed designed to sit in the cabinet and look good, not to be eaten.

I learnt not to order coffee in a shopping mall. Not to buy coffee from a chain or franchise. I learnt to avoid anywhere that spells espresso as 'expresso'. I became wary of anywhere that sold mugaccino (and terrified of anywhere selling potaccino). It seems obvious, now.

I am pretty sure that if a café has a sign that says 'serious coffee' or 'the best coffee in …' or 'obsessively good coffee', then you should beware: it's *not* serious about coffee. This is especially applicable in regional areas with cafés that put the words on sandwich boards out the front. Don't believe them. I often have, and never found it to be the truth.

During that first year in Melbourne, while I was learning to peer from my pushbike into coffee cups and cafés, I was working all over the city. Often the seven o'clock starts on the far side of town were followed by café crawling on the way home, a shower, some writing, then a dinner out, either for work or for personal 'research'.

My real work consisted of shopping centre cooking demonstrations, which nobody wanted to watch, but everybody wanted to sample. Then there was the agency work. There was the hospital where one of the permanent cooks supposedly lit the grill, only for me to find it wasn't lit ten minutes later. A click of the ignition and flames blew out the sides of the hotplate, into my eyeballs, withering most of my lashes and half my eyebrows. We served smoky porridge, and pureed up horrible food into an even more horrible sludge for the infirm. At a kosher nursing home I was roused on not just by the rabbi for mixing up milky and meaty plates (it's a long story) but also by the clients, a formidable bunch of moaners, my only satisfaction being to wake many of them up with a rap on the door in the morning for breakfast. It was a small revenge for their perpetual rudeness, though I always feared someday one of the residents would come up with the ultimate act of defiance, not stirring at all when I knocked.

The worst job of all was at a pub a little way out of the city, where agency chefs were constantly called in. Every shift was shocking. There might have been mouldy schnitzels in the fridge, or fresh meat left out for three days because nobody cared. The aim, in my view, wasn't to worry about the fifty or so meals you'd have to put out forty-five minutes after arriving, it was to try and not poison anybody. The customers weren't fussy, but they wouldn't be long for this world if we didn't check what was to be served. This was the kind of pub where the only thing scarier than the often toothless, abusive and drunk clientele were the rotting chicken parmigiana on trays in the fridge, the slime-green steaks that made you gag as you plucked them from the coolroom and the furry sauces.

The agency work wasn't satisfying. Good restaurant food is one thing, but the stuff we had to slop out made me feel sick to the pit of my stomach. For part of the week I was reviewing for both Melbourne's and Sydney's *Good Food Guides*, and lucky enough to be dining at some of our nation's better eateries. For part of the time I was writing for *Gourmet Traveller*'s restaurant guide, or reviewing cafés for *The Age*, and in between I was cooking food I despised, in places that only cared about the profit margin. The problem was that I needed money.

Reviewing, especially the way I was doing it, over the whole of Victoria, NSW and the ACT, with no car, no savings, and not much of an expense budget, wasn't a very good way to make a living. When I eventually added up most of the jobs and my income, often I'd been working to lose money. *Gourmet Traveller*, for instance, paid an average of $25 per review, with no expenses. I wrote about Canberra and Sydney but lived nearly 700 kilometres away in Melbourne. I stayed in youth hostels or relied on the goodwill of friends and family.

Thankfully I loved doing it, finding it more lifestyle than work, and if I lost money, at least I had been subsidised while I did it. For years being freelance wasn't a good way to make a living, but it was one hell of a way to make a loss.

At that time I wrote for anybody that asked me and for many of those that didn't. I'd send stories to magazines and newspapers based on a whim and a prayer. At one stage I had to borrow money so I could pay to go to a caviar tasting and write a story about it for the *Financial Review*, as well as pay my rent. It was my first tasting of oscietra, beluga and sevruga caviars in one session. More importantly it was my first taste of Dom Pérignon champagne, the cat's pyjamas of fizzy drinks.

What a revelation it turned out to be. As I sipped the delicately beaded champers, and gently pressed the unpasteurised sturgeon roe against the roof of my mouth, popping the sweetly salty beads with my tongue, I had a transcendent experience. For a while I hovered above the room, looking down at others who were tasting, wondering how they could concentrate on mere words in the presence of such perfection. I wondered what it was that they could taste, while I soared above them, dizzy with wonder (not with the grog, it was still early), marvelling at the flavours in my mouth. At once I felt exhilarated and angry, blessed and cheated. Here I was, over thirty years of age, and I'd never known how good these things could be. The Old German Bastard had lied to me when he said that caviar was overrated. My budget had never extended to very much champagne, let alone the Dom. And here I was, tingling with pleasure, having an out-of-body experience over fish eggs and wine, too many years of my life already lost to such pleasure.

For years, subconsciously, I had been testing my palate against others. I found nuances in food that others couldn't. It's not being snobby, it's just innate. My experience of the best restaurants accorded with other reputable reviewers, both here and overseas. But to have the simplest pleasure – fermented grape juice and some fish roe – and be transformed by it, that was another thing altogether.

It was then that I knew I was going to be held hostage by my palate.

I'm a victim of my sense of taste. My father, God love him, is a man to whom most food is good food. And if it's not good, add another pinch of salt to make it good. He doesn't share my ability to sense fragrances or nuances, and he's happy with just about every meal he's ever eaten. I, on the other hand, am often disappointed. I know food can be, and usually should be, better. But I also think there's a god of good things hidden in a meal somewhere, and I'm on a mission to find it.

Being held hostage by your taste is an unusual thing in Australia. In many countries, Thailand perhaps, China, Italy and France, talking about food is not just desirable, it's almost compulsory. Living to eat is commonplace in many nations. But here, where most people eat to live, I have often felt the odd one out.

I have the capacity to taste and remember some flavours. It's a natural thing. I didn't make it up, though I have cultivated the ability through experience and concentration. I don't have the palate memory of wine buffs who can recall not only the winery but the vintage, but I can still taste the fennel roasted in a woodfired oven in Puglia, or Alain Passard's roasted lobster with white beans and coriander at Paris's three Michelin starred L'Arpège, more than a decade later.

I can still taste the metallic nature of the blood that stained a woman's mouth on a hillside in Tassie. She'd fallen from a cliff just before I discovered her, her body slightly crumpled, but the heat still in it. I tried to give her mouth to mouth, and watched as the light slipped from her eyes, the colour from her skin, the heat from her body. For the better part of a day I sat waiting for the chopper to come and take her body down, and for weeks I spat every few minutes, the taste of the last of her life lingering on my tongue.

I can still remember Stephanie's trifle in Melbourne and Must Winebar's roasted chicken in Perth. I can recall with amazing clarity a poached egg on brandade at Sydney's Claude's, the pasta with radicchio and fontina I ate at Melbourne's Café Di Stasio. But I can also never escape the bad flavours; the taste of food I ate just before I fell ill, the rancid fat of dodgy hot chips, or the mineral tang of the life of a woman who never made it home from a bushwalk in Tasmania. With the ability to taste comes pleasure and pain, and with the privilege of being able to convey what you taste in food comes a responsibility to be honest to yourself. The capacity of discernment is a mixed blessing. But it sure helped me later in my career.

A simple request appeared out of the fax one day, asking if I was interested in writing recipes for one of the best-read magazines in the nation, *Good Weekend*, which appeared each Saturday in *The Sydney Morning Herald* and *The Age*. They suggested that I send five sample columns for them to consider. Nearly ten years later I'm still writing for them. A year or so after starting that column, *Gourmet Traveller* asked me to write about products each month. For the first time in a while I actually had a bit of spare money for things like a kitchen table and a lamp. I even bought a second-hand desk and a proper chair to sit at. I also updated my old seven-kilogram laptop to something else second-hand, a computer you actually could carry around without growing arms like a chimpanzee.

Without consciously realising it, as my freelance work began to pile up, I stepped from the kitchen for good. From an impoverished chef with no work I'd become a very busy professional food writer. I was tasting food, road-testing coffee machines, describing dishes in restaurants and co-editing Melbourne's *Cheap Eats and Café Guide*. I was commissioned to write a 70,000-word book on Italian food by Lonely Planet. While the book didn't make me any money after I'd paid for my expenses, I didn't lose much. In the process I travelled to each and every region in Italy, something most Italians have never done. I learnt the importance of knowing your song well before you start singing, of being the person who's been to the source of the produce. Instead of just reading about the food of a place, I wanted to see it with my own eyes, taste it with my own mouth, feel it with my tongue. After three years in Melbourne I was too busy to work out what I needed to do to turn a profit; instead I was immersed in restaurants, in the world's cuisines, in endless short and long trips and several hundred pieces a year (most of them 150 words or less). I had a recipe book contract and there was the suggestion of more work if I moved back to Australia's largest city.

My peripatetic lifestyle was starting to look ridiculous, but pretty soon, for the first time, food writing would start to earn me a living rather than just a lifestyle.

9

A year in Ab Fab

GOD, IT WAS A CHANGE to be popular. Suddenly, I was feted. After being stiffed by an unscrupulous colleague at a Melbourne café guide, I landed in Sydney and won an award. It was judged on early writings, using torn out and photocopied pages roughly hewn from magazines. I sent it hurriedly right on deadline, just on the off-chance. Then, without warning, I became The Food Media Club's Best New Writer, the black-tie award presentation accompanied by a wall-sized projection of my manky clippings. Not for the last time I wished I'd taken more care.

The award came as a bit of a shock. I was just doing what I'd been doing for a few years, but the exposure had the phone ringing. And one call came from a well-respected national magazine, *Vogue Entertaining + Travel*, the original Australian food mag, asking me if I was interested in talking to the editor about a job.

Of course I said no. Why would I be interested in a job, of all things? Jeeesus. I was busy. Too busy, even. My magazine and newspaper work was building up. I was back in Sydney doing what I did best, eating – oh, and writing and cooking. I had a regular column. I had lots of reviews to write for a new café guide, and the *Good Food Guide* coming up as well. Poor as usual, but frantic. So no, I didn't want a job, thanks very much.

Thing is, everybody I mentioned the *Vogue* job to said I had rocks in my head. It's a good magazine. It's national. It has an international profile, and it could, just possibly, pay you MORE THAN YOU'VE EVER BEEN PAID. For travelling and writing about food. Derr.

So I swallowed my pride and rang to say that when I said no, I meant maybe, that I'd love to come in and talk about the job and of course I was always very interested and I must've misheard or misunderstood or just misconstrued what was involved. In other words, I had to do some sucking up.

I got the job. A real, office-based job where you go in, pretend to look busy, and leave. It was brilliant. You could come in hung over, fudge your way through the day, and still they'd unload a barrow load of cash into your bank account each week. After being freelance, it felt like a barrow load, anyway.

And while I did do some fudging, most days I actually worked incredibly hard. The trips — and there were a few — ate into my own time; at one stage I was tasting food till one am then up again at five am for a flight back to the office. I'd be writing recipes in the evenings, or checking out restaurants (with my barrow load of cash), or maybe working with the world's most talented food photographers, turning dross into magazine gold.

Before I started the job, I learnt the Vogue Handshake at an eastern suburbs party. From my limited experience it seems that the main objectives of this kind of party are to call everyone 'darling darling', air kiss with precision and perfect the Vogue Handshake (or more accurately, the Magazine Handshake). The idea is to greet the person you're being introduced to warmly, holding them by the hand – limp-wristed is best, and possibly grasping them by the elbow as well – then gently pulling them towards you. At the same time you scan the room over their shoulder, looking for someone more important, popular, better looking or influential – in short, someone you'd rather be speaking to. You don't make eye contact, heaven forbid, and as you part you say, 'we must catch up, we really must,' but don't exchange telephone numbers, business cards, or even email addresses. 'Mwah, mwah. Yes, we must,' is the correct reply.

Coming from kitchens, where a ponce is called a fucking ponce, I felt not just like a fish out of water, but a baby barramundi gulping for air, ready for the Chinese steamer.

Despite my reservations, I became the magazine's features editor, a role that involved, well, I didn't know what at the time, though I knew it would involve writing about food. It also involved dealing with other writers, coming up with story ideas and reading final copy on page. Ironic, isn't it: from struggling freelancer one week to dealing with struggling freelancers the next.

Freelancers, I learnt, fall into many categories. There are the quiet ones. There are the frantic ones, with story suggestions clogging your phone/fax or email. There are the sucky ones, complete with dinner invitations or lascivious suggestions (ooh err). And there are the painful, pushy, annoying ones. Sadly, from my observations it's those in the last category that get the work, regardless of ability.

Not with me, however. I actually escorted a freelancer from the office during my second week, telling her she had a bad attitude and that I'd rather choke on my own vomit than publish anything of hers, or words to that effect. In my defence she had accused me of stealing story ideas. Actually, I'd *offered* her a story. Anyway, the editor told me, after I explained how I'd just, oh so politely, thrown someone out of the office, that perhaps I should be more diplomatic in future. My kitchen attitude wouldn't pass muster here, obviously. I should've just said we must catch up, we really must. Mwah.

Real jobs are a shock to someone who's been self-employed, let alone to a someone who began his career in kitchens. You can't just sack a person because they're lazy, or incompetent, or spiteful or useless. Apparently. No matter how much you may want to. So the dead wood lingers, nay, floats to the top. You can't hurry people up when they miss deadline, *yet again*, or expect them to work with everybody else, not *against* them. You're not supposed to fall asleep at your desk in that post-lunch haze in an office, either, no matter how quiet it is. Though I did.

My year in a magazine was a cross between *Just Shoot Me* and *Ab Fab*. We even had our own Patsy, a woman whose work ethic was so devoid of scruples, or direction, that she could disappear for days at a time. Perhaps she'd taken an unnecessary week-long trip on the *QEII* or similar, without telling anyone, only to flounce back with a badly written 3000-word story nobody at the magazine wanted, but that the cruise company's PR had been promised would run. Even the job of editing her pieces down to a more manageable 800 words fell to someone else, and invariably – and inexplicably – the stories always ran. In time I came to realise that the stories themselves weren't necessarily that important.

Magazine work introduced me to the real nature of food photography and styling, the things that sell magazines. Thankfully long gone were the days where the hamburger bun was made of plastic, the apple rubbed with oil, the food painted with jelly or sprayed with chemicals to make it look fresh and pert (in that strange, disconcerting way that things look not quite right, similar to plastic surgery).

Australia, by that stage, was teaching the world about food photography, and – editorially at least – it was all edible (bar the occasional plastic ice cube or mashed potato used as ice-cream). Tweaked, fiddled with and overhandled, yes, but real, edible food, with natural light making it look totally scrumptious, as if you could fork it into your mouth straight off the page.

Vogue Entertaining, in its heyday, redefined food photography for the world. Under Sue Fairlie-Cuninghame as both recipe writer and stylist, and with Earl Carter, Quentin Bacon and Geoff Lung as photographers, it became the envy of food magazines everywhere. What we see today is a result of their expression of real food, shot up close and with mostly natural light. *Vogue* was on every other magazine's subscription list, and now, thanks to that, Aussie photographers get gigs around the world, from Martha Stewart titles in the US to *Olive Magazine* in the UK.

Food photography is a fine art. Covers, vital for magazines that rely on newsagent sales, are agonised over. The photographers themselves are carefully selected. Food photographers are the real talent, taking brown, sludgy food and lighting it with flair and style, making the mundane into something gorgeous.

By the time I was at *Vogue*, Sue Fairlie-Cuninghame had moved on, and I was introduced to many dubious food 'stylists' who seemed to be just glorified shoppers; food obsessives with little understanding of cooking at all. A good stylist can be a miracle worker, creating any number of exotic or cosy, homey environments, all within a studio setting, but I was often left wondering at the fact that the stylists (and photographers) earn multiple times what the actual recipe writer earns. It seems (probably because I write recipes) a strange place to put the emphasis.

When it comes to styling, I'm of the more natural school. I want food that looks like real food; pasta that has fallen from the tongs rather than pasta that's been twirled self-consciously around a fork. I want cooked food in cooking dishes and finished food on plates. Sure, work some genius with the light, with the mood. And maybe lash out on the occasional esoteric playful look. But mostly please give me a roasting tray with baked-on bits, give me a dish that at least, in some small way, resembles one that I can cook. Just don't favour styling over substance, that's all I ask. I know it's foolish to think that way. Real food doesn't sell as many cookbooks, it doesn't sell magazines, and it doesn't seem to resonate as much as the unattainable picture that's taken a professional cook, a stylist and a photographer hours to produce. But I still hanker for real food photography.

It must be admitted that I've got little clue about the appropriate look. I had made it to my third interview for the job at *Vogue* when the editor asked me, 'Do you ever wear anything other than T-shirts?' and suggested that as an ambassador for the brand, I may have to actually dress up some time.

Despite my lack of style, in this job I instantly had much more credibility. Matthew Evans the writer who was passed over for lots of things became Matthew Evans who people were gagging to have at their functions. Invitations filled the mail. PR firms had my number. I drank litres of good wine. There was seemingly no end to the pulling power of this job, be it from those looking for regular work, offering any number of favours, to those looking to promote their products. From invisible I suddenly became too visible for my own comfort – and all the while being treated as an authority. The curious thing is that I immediately garnered more respect, making compromises that I wouldn't have countenanced just a few weeks earlier, than I did being freelance and ethically sound.

The editor split work time between this magazine and another. There was no deputy, however, and the day-to-day management fell somewhere between myself and the others in the team. I use the word 'team' loosely. It was more a group of people who sometimes worked in the same office, with disparate ideas of what constituted a good story, all doing their own thing with little direction. A kitchen 'team' at least all tried to put out meals at an appropriate time. A magazine team seemed to be pulling in opposite directions, bitching about each other, sometimes within hearing, and undermining each other – luckily with very little efficiency. At least you knew a chef didn't like you when he pegged a frying pan at your head. In an office, you were never quite sure who the enemy was. 'Take your chair to lunch,' was the joke, the idea being that if you did, you'd still have somewhere to sit when you came back in. Staff regularly departed at very short notice from some magazine offices.

The editor had built up the magazine to a point where about a quarter of all its sales were international. It had a reputation by being edgy, worthy, and aspirational. The downside of this was that she worked so hard that it was difficult to get hold of her. She didn't just avoid confrontation, she seemed to avoid contact. Many were the times you'd be at your desk and not know where she was or what she was doing. Communication was uncommon.

I took a trip to London based on a meeting months before where we discussed a story idea, only to find out on the night prior to flying out that they couldn't be sure they'd want the story. Apparently someone had just jagged free accommodation in London and we'd be doing a big hotel feature instead. My trip was all booked. I went, I took a photographer. We paid our own expenses, including flights and hotels and restaurants, shot and wrote the story. But as far as I know it never appeared in print.

Working at *Vogue* was a brilliant opportunity, though. I travelled the Eastern Orient Express, stayed at the Peninsula Hotel, and drank my body weight in champagne on several occasions. I should've screwed as much as possible out of the job, taken the cruises, the free ski trips and resort reviews. Instead I wanted to publish a story giving 101 things to do in Sydney during the Olympics, even though it was predominantly at my own expense.

I wanted to do stories on Lapland and Turkey, stories that took a lot more putting together.

Interestingly for a travel magazine, there was no budget for me to travel. Call me naïve, but it seems a little strange to be told you can only travel for a story if someone else pays. Tourism authorities, perhaps? Tour organisers, maybe? As the food editor for a national magazine told me recently, 'if it's a free trip, it's a story we don't want.'

When I started at the magazine, travel industry types laughed about how blatantly we scammed airfares and free hotels, and how most of the time the trips were for management or frou frou rather than a story. At one stage I spent two weeks of my time just trying to get a free airfare for a story I thought the magazine should run, rather than a story it was just handed on a plate. The difficulty with just using free trips is that the stories are always the same — cruising, Noosa, hotels you can't afford to stay in, spas. Yawn. Yes they may be worthy stories, but not every issue. Buying the fare at cost — an equitable way that wouldn't compromise editorial standards — would have been the equivalent of two days' wages. You can see why free trips might win out.

What's even more surprising, at least to this food tragic, is that for a food and travel title they didn't have a budget for dining out, either. Certainly not one that I could access, and I wrote the restaurant news stories each month. Magazines have long had problems with credibility. When I was on staff — and let's be clear about this, *at a food and travel magazine no less* — we were expected to take up offers of free meals. We didn't visit restaurants unannounced or pay our own way.

Although they might look the same to the reader, there are big differences in ethics and credibility from publication to publication. Some magazine editors are in it for the kudos. They want to be popular, they want the attention when they dine out. They love the free wine dinners, the Bolly. Yes, sweetie darling, the snout in the trough mentality is alive and well and living in a magazine near you. At the time of writing, a Sydney-based food magazine ran a story on Newcastle and was sponsored to go. It's a couple of hours' drive at most. It's just up the road, for crying out loud. The magazine is owned by one of the wealthiest companies in the nation. And they have to be *sponsored* to go?

I came to all my jobs as a chef who loved to eat and travel. I didn't expect the free meal, the free ride, though I did love the perks, thanks very much. But what troubled me was that I'd thought magazines published stories because they believed in them, not because someone bought the back page as an advertiser then pressured the magazine to give them editorial coverage. I didn't expect moral bankruptcy.

Don't get me wrong, I still subscribe to food magazines and read them avidly. Magazines gave me a start when I needed it. They inspired me to stay cooking when I was being abused and working with food you wouldn't want to feed your dog. I still find it therapeutic flicking through them and seeing what they have to say about produce, places and people. But I punch the page when they have an overcooked crème caramel on the cover (you can tell from the bubbles up the side), promote ingredients that aren't in season or rave about a product that you can tell is outside their normal realm of interest, probably because there's been pressure from advertising. I rant about stories that are afraid to criticise, or that criticise but can't be trusted because the magazines they appear in don't have the moral high ground. Yet they want you to believe their views.

Restaurant Magazine in the UK wants us to trust its annual 'World's 50 Best Restaurants' list, but until I wrote about them in 2006, they didn't even ask that their judges had been to the restaurants. Ever. Let alone in the previous twelve months. And they certainly don't pay most people's expenses. How do I know? Because I have been asked to vote for the list, and I know of people who've voted for restaurants they've never been to. In 2007 they finally changed the ruling so judges had to have visited any restaurant they vote for within the last eighteen months.

The good news is that the payola for advertisers does seem to have become more open and honest in recent years with the advent of 'news from our sponsors' pages towards the back of magazines. Reviews seem to be less than totally favourable, an indication that they're not on the take, and free trips often openly declared. But as long as some in the industry take the moolah, the freebies and the indiscretions in their stride – writing stories as they go – it makes the rest of us look compromised.

Perhaps I was the odd one out in my attitude to professionalism and ethics. Maybe I was too concerned with stuff that is just not that interesting to the readers. But I did wonder if perhaps there wasn't room for concerned food journalism that was as exciting as it was accurate, as credible as it was inspirational. Advertisers paid our wages, but surely readers deserved objective reports? I didn't wonder for long. I was about to launch into the most credible, authoritative and respected role in food journalism in the country. And the most bitched about.

10

The free lunch

WHAT YOU'VE HEARD is true. Reviewing restaurants is
the best job in the world. It's ten times as good as you
can imagine, yet less glamorous than you've ever considered. Well, it was for me. It surpassed my expectations
in many respects, left me speechless, mesmerised and in
awe. It also disappointed me when I least expected it to.
It left me with chest pain and weight gain; it left me perse-
cuted, popular, defamed, sued, ecstatic and appreciated.
But in spite of it all, it is probably the best work you can
do sitting up.

A review doesn't appear because the restaurant wants it.
It doesn't get published because reviewers need someone to
subsidise their lifestyle. A restaurant review exists because
the public demand it.

Most restaurant 'reviews' you see, however, are not really
reviews as such. They're compromised. Often they're in the
local paper on the same page as the ad for the restaurant.
Some annual guidebooks don't even make yearly visits to
the restaurants they write about. Smaller newspapers are
often sponsored or have been given a free meal in return
for some coverage. On tight budgets, with no resources,
smaller publications resort to the simplest, cheapest way to

review, which is of dubious benefit to the reader — you're hardly going to criticise the people who pay your bills. Most of the bigger publications, however, pay their way. That way, reviewers are free to write without being unnecessarily encumbered.

I'd been a chef and recipe writer, a voracious consumer of other people's views and reviews for years. Even as an apprentice I'd written to the local paper to complain about the quality of reviewers after one journalist used words to the effect of 'apparently coriander is a common herb in Thai cookery', followed up with this piece of wisdom: 'the only difference between good and bad food is that good food doesn't make you sick'.

Many newspapers send the lowly trainee, the cadet, out to do restaurant reviews because they don't get paid much and need the free meal. What the reader gets are the thoughts of an inexperienced writer and diner. Someone's business is in the hands of a person who probably hasn't eaten out much, or written much. In this way newspapers shaft restaurants in a way they wouldn't any other small business.

Professional restaurant reviewing may seem like a contradiction in terms. But to do the job properly, to give the dining public an experienced, credible, readable choice it's better to have someone dedicated to the task, not just doing it between PR gigs or advertising copy. A full-time reviewer knows the industry, its movements, its foibles, its high and low points. How can you take responsibility for a chef's hat award, something that can cost or make the business many tens if not hundreds of thousands of dollars, if you haven't been immersed in the industry as a diner?

The Sydney Morning Herald's chief restaurant critic was a position I'd long wondered about. Influential, respected, and based in a dynamic dining city still on the ascendant, it seemed the duck's guts of reviewing jobs. With up to a million readers a week, and the supposed ability to make or break a restaurant, it's often considered the only serious, properly critical and discerning review in town. To many people, including myself, it seemed like the perfect job. But over the years I'd watched the incumbent, Terry Durack. I'd been making a living writing about food, eating in the best restaurants, cooking at home, working for a range of publications, without any of the angst that he had. I knew of legal letters, organised revolts by chefs and suggestions of bias and favouritism that rippled through the restaurant community. And as I watched, I could see the downside of the job.

A reviewer makes enemies. A reviewer has to stand up and voice an opinion they can back up in a society that often thinks passionate, honest talk about food is the stuff of wankers. They must know the city, its people and its restaurants. A reviewer has to trawl the suburbs, the CBD, the state for restaurants, and convey passion and disappointment on a weekly basis. They must know food, and it helps if they understand how it's cooked.

Part of me felt tinged with guilt for considering doing a role where it's all too easy to criticise. Not only that, but criticising chefs, who do one of the hardest jobs imaginable. Reviewers, however, need to show no fear or favour of household names. In a country that obsesses over its celebrity chefs, the role of the reviewer is to debunk the myths and praise only where it's due, regardless of the restaurateur's reputation. Incumbent high-profile chefs, of course, don't like that. And they hold the attention of not only the public, but an often pliable food media, too.

Knowing too much about the industry almost put me off doing the job. The people reviewers write about each week are the very orcs and trolls that I'd worked with. By the time the *SMH* gig came up, I was ensconced in my role at *Vogue*, writing only positive things about good producers and restaurants.

When the newspaper rang me to say that Terry Durack had resigned and they thought I might like to apply for the job, I didn't want it. Who goes out of their way to make enemies? I certainly wasn't afraid, just comfortable in a less high-profile role.

I'd seen the dark heart of restaurant kitchens, I knew the tricks they had with the food. I'd looked into the eyes of evil restaurateurs, been scammed, poisoned, and verbally abused. And yet there's something so incredibly attractive about restaurants and the joy of sharing a good place when you find it that I found utterly compelling. I adored every- thing about eating out and wanted to scream a good restaurant's praises from the highest roof. And the highest roof in Australia is as reviewer for *The Sydney Morning Herald*. Like it or not, the job has cachet.

I met with two editors, lunching on a splendid seafood meal overlooking the water with the city as backdrop. I considered the role, its antagonistic nature, what it would mean, how I would do it, what it would involve physically, emotionally, financially.

And eventually I succumbed. Along with other potential

reviewers I visited a new restaurant, wrote my review, scored it, and sent it in. Each writer's piece, including Durack's review of the same restaurant, was laid out on a page. The pages were circulated, without by-lines, and the *Herald*'s section editors rated them.

Perhaps remarkably, considering my own reservations, I won the job, taking a pay cut to do so. Just another dickhett from Canberra was handed a gig writing about the best restaurants in the land. A paid gig at that. Despite an industry background, I wanted to be the bloke reviewing for regular and rare diners alike, never for the chefs, never for the other food media.

And while I thought I knew what it entailed, I'd only imagined half of it. Nobody told me back then about court cases, world-class bitchiness and egos as puffed as soufflés, let alone the threats of Eastern European mafia or the jealousy of other food journalists. There was no talk then of my own newspaper investigating me, the chest pain I'd suffer during the worst of it, the backstabbing, gossip mongering, vitriolic blog writing and sheer volume of work. I was just an ordinary bloke from an average back-ground who was going to be paid to voice his opinion. His honest opinion.

At *The Sydney Morning Herald*, journalistic integrity seemed to count for something. Nobody could pressure me to say or not say anything, within the boundaries of the law and good taste. It was to be the most liberating and exhilarating time yet, full of thrills and angst, pain and pleasure, along with the most amazing meals a bloke could ever expect to eat. And this time, most of the time, the boss was paying.

I stepped from a hectic, well-travelled, full-on life as a low-key but mildly successful food writer into a whirlwind that engulfed the next half a decade. Part of that whirlwind was because of the catch that comes with the *SMH* chief critic's job: co-editorship of *The Good Food Guide*. The annual restaurant guide is three hundred pages of anguish, detail and pain. It's also the most authoritative book of its kind in the state.

The combined roles of co-editor and chief reviewer make the job relatively important and high profile. And with profile comes responsibility and controversy.

The role of a reviewer, of course, is to criticise. It is by its very nature adversarial. Imagine how happy you'd be in your job if someone came through and criticised the way you did your filing, the state of the windows and your manner on the telephone.

Being reviewed is a horrid experience, like having the auditors in. I think of it as like looking in a mirror under fluorescent lights. You suddenly see your own flaws, failings that perhaps you knew about but didn't ever really admit consciously. They're exposed in a harsh way, with no place to hide. It's uncomfortable, and trust me, it can be difficult from both sides.

Maybe I took the responsibility too seriously. In my first year as a restaurant reviewer I ate out 540 times for work. I also ate out for pleasure, even though there weren't many meal times left outside work hours.

Before the job started I flew myself to China and ate like a madman: goose, cobra heart, pork a thousand ways, turtle, hairy crab, a million dumplings. I wanted to immerse myself in one of the world's great cuisines, one that resonates in

Sydney, and one that I'd neglected to cover as well as I had Thai, Italian or French. It's important that the public has a reviewer they can trust on a range of cuisines.

The trust of the public is something I hope I earned in my time as reviewer. Credibility and trust is a gift not easily given and yet like virginity is so easily lost. There's no room for endless narratives about the reviewer's life with no description of the food and just a score unjustified in the words. In Australia, both the media outlets and the public want a certain level of expertise and description delivered with their opinions. It can make for a duller read, but a more trustworthy read, I hope.

There's also a sting with the profile. Although you bear a great weight of responsibility on your shoulders as a (hopefully) well-respected, credible voice, in Australia the reviews are namby-pamby compared to those in Britain. No analogies with a minke whale's haemorrhoids or compost in this country. Our tight defamation laws (and the way newspapers interpret them) take the bite out of reviews, and the fun. Thanks to two very expensive defamation cases won by restaurants prior to Durack's tenure, the lawyers will want to know not just when you previously ate compost, but also why.

Defamation is tricky territory to navigate, and the legal team at the newspaper know it as well as anyone. Reviews can have an impact on a restaurant, but I reckon legal action is an example of shooting the messenger. I don't believe a negative review can close a restaurant unless it was already on shaky ground. Both restaurants that sued my predecessors are still trading more than a decade later. A reviewer is like a friend who eats out a lot, someone you can turn to for advice. Or not, if you don't like what they've got to say. They're not the bank, the landlord or the regular customer, who are more likely to have an impact on the success of a business.

But legal intervention means the views of a restaurant critic are watered down. Reviews, once legalled, are stripped of the richness of the English language (think whale's haemorrhoids, compost) and become more anodyne, full of 'nice' words with meanings other than the one intended. To fully understand them, you almost need a dictionary of terms.

Cheap and cheerful? That probably means 'dodgy'.

Aims at …? Misses.

Modest? Ramshackle, perhaps, or run down.

Not to my tastes? Utter crap.

Anonymous? Offensive in the extreme merely by being dull.

Distracted? Lazy.

Enthusiastic? Eager but untrained.

Aloof? Arrogant.

Restrained? Boring.

Ambitious? A failure.

Showy? Full of wankers screaming into their mobiles and thinking they're important.

Heavy? Disgustingly thick.

Rich? First heart attack material.

Indulgent? Pass the defibrillator and stand back.

The real loser is the diner, who seldom gets an accurate picture. Mediocre restaurants are made to sound pleasant. Lacklustre restaurants are absent. Seriously crap places don't make it into print because the publishers can't afford the legal bills.

I'm a great believer in having strong, workable defamation laws, but having seen how they inhibit the work of a restaurant reviewer, I don't think ours do the public any favours. Thanks to the high cost and the high risk, there's a paucity of worthwhile, critical reviews in our major cities. Food is sexy, restaurants are the new clubs and chefs the new rock stars, but the public is let down by the reviews they're allowed to read.

Reviewing restaurants is easy. It's much like going out to dinner, really. You visit a restaurant, eat, drink, pay and leave. The only proviso is that you have to remember it all, or take notes or photos and write about it later.

Often a reviewer gives a score, and it's no secret formula, at least at the publications I worked on. A restaurant could get 10 points for food, 5 for service, 3 for ambience and 2 for a sprinkling of magic. The magic could be a world-class view, incomparable flavours underpinned by astonishing ideas, or a waiter who set new standards for the profession. Out of 20 points most places scored around 13 or 14. In other words, average. For most of them that's a good score. It's not world class (for which 18 and above was required) and it's not a fail. These were decent businesses doing a decent job.

Very few restaurants scored below 12 when I reviewed, and only three out of 250 failed completely. Such a high-profile review comes with a huge amount of responsibility. That, combined with those strict defamation laws, meant failing restaurants was something we did rarely and only in the public interest. I'm aware that plenty of people love reading about dodgy restaurants, applauding a reviewer for putting the boot in. But negative reviews weren't the ones I wanted to be judged on (though it seems those are the ones that last – at the time of writing I still have a defamation case before the courts).

The score has to be seen in context. I didn't start the system but I liked it. It gives enough scope to rate Australia's amazing restaurants highly, on a world scale, without failing decent also-rans. Scores out of 10 seem too tight and need half points; out of 100 and you can't really be sure a 72 isn't a 75. Out of 20 seems just right without being ridiculous. The idea is to give options. For many diners a 14 out of 20 restaurant should be good enough. Not everybody has the experience, the money, or the desire to go to a higher scoring restaurant. Some can't taste the difference in the food, and there's nothing to be ashamed of in that. Hey, some of my family are in that category. A review may talk about nuances in food that some people can't taste, such as the incredible but fleeting flavour of rosewater granita drizzled with champagne at MG Garage. That's okay. Being discerning comes more naturally to some people than others. Some people can perceive more from a plate of food, a glass of wine, and probably the scent of a rose, than others. Part of it is genetic, part upbringing and culture. I make no apologies for writing for the discerning, but I was also conscious that everybody has their level.

A high-scoring restaurant isn't for everybody for many reasons. Some people don't like having too many waiters lapping serviettes, pouring the wine and constantly checking up on them. Some diners don't want fancy food, it's just not their way; they're happier with tumblers for their BYO and paper napkins. And there's nothing wrong with that either – I'm a great fan of it myself. For others, quality is judged by the quantity, not by flavour.

There's a restaurant for everyone, and every circumstance. I adore going to the flashiest places for an occasion. Other times I just want someone else to cook. And often I'm after somewhere local, decent, affordable and with staff who make me feel loved. That, after all, is the best restaurant for most people, most of the time. What differs is how you define local, affordable, and decent.

Our scoring system favours the food. Why? Because food has long been Australia's weakest point. Blame it on the fact that we inherited the worst of English cookery, but we didn't have a cuisine to be proud of. Not our own, not an imported or borrowed cuisine. Nothing. Fortunately, that has changed drastically over the last two decades and our restaurants have played a pivotal role in giving us food that rates well on any scale.

People go out to eat. That's the point of going out. Yes, they do get served, and watered, but they go out to be fed. Is the score I used too food heavy? You could argue it is, especially when most diners will go out to find good food, but will only return based on good service. But with thousands of restaurants to choose from, you can always find a bad meal on your own. As a service to those who care, reviews are written for those who want better food than they already know, and better options than they already have. Good service depends somewhat on the personality of not just the waiter, but also the diner, and how the two interact. Good food is a matter of craft, not personality. And thank God for that.

I'm actually sympathetic to both restaurants and diners, having been on both sides of the swing doors. I don't have a lot of time for the 'I can cook it at home for much less' crowd who believe paying for a meal out is, by its very nature, overly excessive.

Yes, you can cook food at home. You can also cut your own hair, paint your own house, milk your own cows and rear and slaughter your own pigs. But I bet you don't.

Price is relative. A restaurant provides you with a (hopefully) clean space, often with lovely designer touches you don't have at home. They have someone come to your table and wait upon you, someone to cook your food to order and someone to wash up after you've gone. Restaurants also have rent, insurance and serial thieves – known as customers – who nick everything that isn't nailed down.

The majority of restaurants that I reviewed had better glassware than most houses, better crockery and cutlery, better heating and air-conditioning. Many had far better locations, crisp white linen, a cellar of some note, fresher produce and people cooking with far more skill than you and I have. Yet the average restaurant profit hovers around 3 per cent per annum.

One of my lawyers costs $38.50 for six minutes' work. I have never been to her office, she doesn't have to clean up after me or keep me warm for three hours at a table and chair that the firm provides. She certainly doesn't make me feel loved. My masseur costs $70 for a table and a rub, no fresh ingredients, no choice of menu, no view and only minimal training. So don't tell me eating out is too expensive. The mark-up on shoes, perfume and sandwiches is far bigger than on restaurant food. A restaurant may be out of your budget, so choose somewhere simpler or, better still, cook a meal you can trust from scratch at home. It only takes about twenty minutes to whip up the perfect pasta. What's your hourly rate?

During my time at the *SMH*, eating out was my life. About ten mealtimes a week, I would rub my hands together glee-fully in that marvellous moment between ordering and the first food arriving. Friends would laugh, but I loved the anticipation of a great meal – and I always anticipated a great meal, despite much experience to the contrary. To me, this time was happy hour. Every restaurant had the poten-tial to outperform expectations, to surprise, delight, thrill and excite. Every meal out was a revelation, and I was optimistic at every chance.

All this time I also cooked at home, testing for a recipe column, at least one recipe a week and usually more. In between times I'd be entertaining at home as often as my schedule allowed. Friends would arrive for a meal that could stretch leisurely over four hours and include ten courses.

I adored having people around for a meal, and after so much eating out the act of cooking was therapeutic. Stirring a risotto, crushing garlic, hand rolling pasta or pressing buttery shortcake mixture into a tin all felt wonderfully liberating. Whilst I had yardstick restaurants that I'd visit to recalibrate my tastebuds, it was home cooking that proved to be the best antidote to restaurants and the best place for me to be myself without the glare of notoriety and recognition.

✻

For a decade I ate across Australia, everywhere from Vietnamese pho joints to the finest of fine diners. I submerged myself in restaurant culture as a customer rather than as a chef, rejoicing in good flavours, intrigued by the stellar technique of so many chefs, exultant about my finds, saddened when restaurants let me down or failed to match my expectations. Every meal, I hoped, was to be the best meal of my life.

Sometimes I was blown away. When Peter Gilmore moved from a northern beaches restaurant to the harbourside fine diner, Quay, I could scarcely believe how good the flavours had become. With a bigger team, this extraordinarily talented (and strangely nice) chef played with textures like an artist, using an almost Chinese palate. Yet the English language, at a restaurant like this, seemed desperately lacking. The Chinese have several words for crisp (think of the differences between iceberg lettuce, pork crackling, Peking duck skin and pastry) where we just have one or two. The Japanese describe *umami*, the mouth-filling flavour of food from amines and glutamates, where English has no words to adequately address it.

It was the same at Marque, where Mark Best created food that made the hairs stand on the back of my neck, where I've wept at the flavours in a dish. English, or at least my ability to use it, seemed such a faint reflection of the dishes themselves. I strove to express the joy found in a perfectly seared piece of John Dory at est. under the hands of Peter Doyle, the immaculately presented series of dishes at Tetsuya's, the sheer genius and aesthetics of sushi master Yoshii Ryuichi, or the incredible woodfired cuisine at the Blue Mountains' Vulcans. Having swooned over

Rockpool's lobster tagine and Sean Moran's anything at Sean's Panaroma, I found myself straining to make the experience sound as good in print as it had been in person. I'd use analogies to music, to emotions, to sex, but all seemed woefully inadequate compared to eating the meal for yourself.

Happily, the reviews had an incredible response in terms of where people chose to eat, so at least the public could then enjoy the same delight I'd had – if they could put up with the queues. At Thai exponents Spice I Am, the usual twenty-minute wait for a table – at what was little more than a noodle bar – blew out to three hours. And they only got 14 out of 20.

At a café called Carabella, punters showed up with the newspaper in hand, demanding tables, pretending to be mates with the owner, calling out 'G'day Ricky', to the first waiter they saw and trying to order dinner items I'd suggested, but at lunchtime. Carabella scored 13.

A strangely empty but wonderful fish bistro, Billingsgate, went from losing a couple of thousand dollars a week before being reviewed, to being booked up a month in advance after getting 14 out of 20, all captured beautifully on a documentary that I'd become a bit player in.

The ability of the reviewer to make a restaurant popular, at least for a few weeks, was astonishing. The sad thing was how fickle the dining public was, and how many great restaurants would end up empty a few months after opening. Sydney's shiny crowd often showed no loyalty and flocked to the next bright new thing like moths. The positive thing about this is that it gives newcomers a chance, but on the downside it leaves many remarkable restaurants to die a slow death. After an 18 out of 20 review at est., Peter Doyle was booked out most lunches and dinners for a year. And yet his previous two restaurants, Cicada and Celsius, struggled to make money before they closed.

Week after week, I looked to find good dining options for the people of Sydney. Despite only three restaurants failing out of about 250 published newspaper reviews, I was variously accused of 'carping negativity', having a 'churlish' nature, a 'scathing, sarcastic' tone and an 'acid tongue'. I visited many more crap restaurants than I bagged. Many, *many* more. Yet still there was a perception that I was hard on restaurants. Hard on smart-arsed restaurants that didn't match up to the hype, yes. And never afraid of the big names in the industry, either. I wasn't afraid of a stoush. I called a shocker a shocker, overused the words *dreary* and *dire* and took on both reputable names and new restaurants alike. I also downgraded complacent or simply inconsistent established places.

But I wanted every restaurant to succeed, willing them on to better things, looking for goodness when, often, there wasn't much. I usually chose dishes that sounded like they'd work and that I'd like, only rarely challenging the chef to prove a bias unfounded. The vast majority of dud restaurants were never written about. It's poor form to slag off a family trattoria in the suburbs when you hold so much public trust in your hands.

It's a shame that you can't just say what you mean, however. The lawyers took out the word *disgusting*, rephrased *overcooked*, weren't keen on 'I'd rather run my tongue around the plughole in the shower than eat this.'

That phrase hit the cutting room floor like many other comments on quality. Even with the lawyers' watchful eyes, a lawsuit is never far away.

When the reviews hit the paper, there was a range of responses, from the predictable to the frightening. Most chefs kept quiet, licking their wounds in their dismally small and badly lit kitchens, perhaps taking some criticism on board, ignoring other bits. The majority of reviews were notable for one thing: a lack of response direct to me. Chefs talked about the reviews, but they didn't talk to me.

Many were the restaurateurs who felt I had personal bias, that I held a grudge, or had 'an issue' with them. Funnily enough, these all had one thing in common; they'd all had lukewarm or negative reviews. My editor, bless him, began to think of me every time he heard the words 'personal bias' and 'vendetta'. It's flattering to me, but perhaps a little egotistical of chefs, to think that I had the time or the energy to care about them as individuals.

Now, as then, I have a responsibility to act honestly and in the interests of the reader, but to care about chefs as people? Come on, I know the industry too well to give a rat's arse about them as people. Their job is to cook, mine to visit their restaurants and give an honest opinion. That's it.

11

Good evening sir,
is that a slug on your top lip?

SERVICE FOR THE dining public is one thing. But what's it like when you're the restaurant critic for 'Good Living'? Part of the problem for a high-profile critic is managing to remain anonymous. For a start, if you're a seasoned diner (as is expected of a reviewer), you'll already be known to some restaurants. Give it a week, a month or a year and all those waiters who spied you at one place will have moved on, pointing you out at new restaurants. It increases exponentially. If they don't pick you on a first visit – and they all have a picture somewhere – a good restaurant will be switched on enough to recognise the name on your credit card. I tried to get a card in another name, and was knocked back for legal reasons. Yet, despite the fact that my picture was published, and I ended up having my dial on telly, well over half the places I reviewed for the newspaper still had no idea who I was.

The game at the others – and it does become a game: restaurants as players, reviewers as umpires – is to try and slip under the radar as often as possible, for as long as possible. It's not just how you're treated, but more importantly how it changes once you're recognised. A professional books under an assumed name so if nothing else they arrive unannounced, if not always remaining unrecognised for the whole meal. As computers have helped restaurants keep track of their customers' dining habits, they've also allowed them to spy on reviewers. When I'd ring a restaurant, they'd record the contact details. If I ever used that name or that telephone number again, they'd know I was coming. They'd know what I ate and when. After a while, they started to recognise my voice. And my friends' voices. And I'd run out of phone numbers where they could call to reconfirm.

It's not as bad in Australia as it is overseas. Ruth Reichl in her book *Garlic and Sapphires* talks about being recognised on a plane, three months before she even became *The New York Times* restaurant reviewer. Frank Bruni, a Reichl successor still at *The New York Times*, has his picture, his credit card names, his aliases and his telephone numbers all listed on a sheet of paper that's handed from restaurant to restaurant. They know when he goes out of town and when he comes back, how he talks to staff and his demeanour. It's scary stuff. Sometimes I felt I was being paranoid, but it seems you can't be too careful when it comes to names, telephone numbers and anonymity.

I used plenty of different names. My middle name. My street name. My partner's name, my sister's boyfriend's name, my other sister's married name. I used the names of the people I dined with, my friends' names, complete strangers' names and made-up phone numbers, and on it went. At one stage I found it impossible to remember the monikers I was using for each restaurant. I remember standing at the front desk of Chairman & Yip in Canberra, a restaurant I'd visited forty or so times, saying I had a booking for Davis. No, Holt. Perhaps Benson? Wilson? Can I have a look at what bookings you do have?

When the restaurant knows you're coming it can skew things for a critic. It's less important if you're recognised once you've arrived; things are already in motion. The veal jus takes hours to make so it's already in place before you walk in the door. The seafood they serve can be no better than that which is in the fridge. The terrines are all made, the confit cured, the pork belly slow roasted. The staff can't get a personality transplant, the vegetables can't be made to be any fresher, and, importantly, the cooking skills of the chef can't improve. All the restaurant can change is the style of service to some extent (though you still can't make a dud waiter into a leading light) and keep a closer eye on the food. Knowing you're coming, on the other hand, means a restaurant can roster on the best waiters, manage the sauces more carefully and buy the seafood the very same morning.

But the thing that happens most when you're recognised is the reverse of what the restaurant expects. They panic. At Marque, a waitress who I'd heard poured the wine with the effortless grace of a ballerina lost her nerve and suddenly dribbled it all over the cloth and my lap. A pleasant maître d' can become an obnoxious know-it-all, fussing and pandering, overly familiar and lingering too long at table. Instead of the kitchen team humming along and serving the food, the whole show can come to a standstill while the reviewer's meal is plated. Sometimes it's cooked a second time if the chef isn't happy. The restaurant may serve bigger portions – probably the last thing an overfed critic wants. And what the reviewer experiences is a team on edge, food that's slow (or that other tables' food is slow, which they'll see if they're watching the dining room), and no chance to enjoy the meal between obsequious visits from the owner, the chef, the sommelier, the floor manager and everybody else who wants to suck up. In short, being recognised is horrid. The vacuous attempt at sincerities may seem pleasant to others. But if you're a normal person who loves to eat out and mind your own business, it's a hollow niceness. Encountered all too often, it has no benefit for the review, and only diminishes the pleasure of the experience.

As another critic once claimed, being recognised means you can have so many people hanging around the table it feels like you're having open-heart surgery. In my view, the reviewer should be passive. I didn't send food back unless it was likely to cause food poisoning. I didn't demand the best table, and I certainly didn't need any free food and drink. My role was as an observer.

Not that all reviewers see it this way. Some may revel in the attention, some seek it or desire it. But to me it stank of insincerity. I knew the chef had probably rubbed the steak against his arse to spite me, so no amount of pandering and over-servicing was going to make me feel loved.

After doing the job for eighteen months, the recognition factor seemed insurmountable. Waiters move jobs with frightening regularity and it only took one swipe of the credit card before switched-on restaurants knew me by sight.

I would get around this in various ways. I would meet my guests after they'd been seated, letting them give a verdict on how quickly the drinks arrived, how comfortable they were made to feel and how the room was worked.

Over time I did alter my appearance. I changed my hair by growing it longer or cutting it severely short, which gave me a few minutes' or hours' grace at some restaurants. I did disguise myself as an older, greyer, fatter man over the five years. But at 194 centimetres tall, about six foot four, I was pretty hard to conceal. I did, however, go into serious disguise to check out a restaurant's attitude.

At the intimate restaurant Claude's in Woollahra, they'd open the discreet door to the press of the buzzer, recognising me immediately every time. I'd use names such as Windsor, or Keating or Soprano, just for a laugh. Once, after they'd challenged me to wear a disguise, they opened the door to a tall, pudgy man in a black wild man wig and beard made of nylon, which sold for about $2 at toy stores. A waiter I'd never met before stood, smiled, and politely asked me what name I had a booking in. They were as professional as ever, even with some crazy at the threshold.

The staff at Otto Ristorante had a reputation for looking after the well-heeled and the well-known. After I reviewed them, I received a complaint that suggested I got better service than the average punter. I was recognised during the visit, but I could see the whole room, and nobody seemed neglected or neglectful. Yet a niggling doubt remained. Was the reader's complaint an isolated incident? Were there two levels of care at Woolloomooloo's swank Italian eatery?

To find out, I had to go back and not be known. It took several hours with the students and staff at Annandale's

College of Make-up and Special Effects, but the disguise was so good even my dog didn't know me. I hardly recognised myself when they'd finished. I had new sunspots and a suit. I carried an extra twenty kilograms in weight and an extra twenty years, plus facial hair, a limp and a gruff attitude.

I walked into Otto nervous as hell about my disguise and yet nobody, not even the friends I met, could tell who I was. The staff didn't notice the fact I couldn't eat much as my disguise loosened around my mouth. I broke into a nervous sweat when I locked eyes with the sommelier, someone I'd known since Canberra days, but he turned away without recognising me (or seeing my beard pull from my face). For two hours I sat behind enemy lines and didn't get noticed. It was brilliant stuff.

And what did it feel like to be Bruce Average, dining at a place known to have more than its fair share of celebrities? Pretty bloody good actually.

Otto's seasoned staff flitted and chatted and darted. They were oblivious to status, joking with couples and groups of all ages and backgrounds, offering a torch for a couple to read with, taking the time to look after everyone's needs.

We arrived towards the end of the rush, and the only difference in service between being Matthew Evans, Restaurant Reviewer, and being the person I became for that night was marginally less attention towards the end of the meal. We had to be a little more proactive as the restaurant wound down to get our final wine order taken. That was it. Despite my panic attacks every time the staff came near, especially those I clearly recognised, it was plain sailing. We felt nurtured, cared for and, if not quite loved, certainly well liked.

The masquerade was worth it. Not because I caught Otto out, but rather because I caught them in. It turned out you didn't have to be the restaurant reviewer for *The Sydney Morning Herald* to get good service at one of the city's consistently hottest spots. You just had to make a booking.

12

A consuming profession

WHILE NEWSPAPER REVIEWS had an impact, there was also the annual guidebook, *The Good Food Guide*, to consider. Remarkably, positive or negative newspaper reviews usually only stayed in the public consciousness for a month. (Unless the restaurant sued, of course, guaranteeing that conversation around Sydney's water coolers would see their name crop up again as the restaurant that'd been poorly reviewed.) *The Good Food Guide* was arguably more influential than the newspaper. Getting awards in the *Guide* was, for many, important not just for increased business success, but for a chef's ego, too. I know from the chef's hat award we won when I was at The Republic in Canberra.

The launch of the book is big news each year, the results always difficult to keep under wraps. The book lasts a year; the newspaper is thrown away the same day, and while one gave some clues as to the other, they often said things quite differently. We also kept some major decisions for the book to expose.

Forgive the pun, but the reviewer's job, at least the way I did it, was all-consuming. The yearly volume had 400 scored restaurants. In addition there were other entries such as cafés and bars, and by the time I left there were

800 entries covering interstate as well as local restaurants, plus provedores and wineries. I found *The Good Food Guide* eats up as many hours as you can give it, still demanding more. With constant changes as the book goes to press, your job is never done. You actually pray for the axe of the deadline to fall, saving you from the inevitable and endless revising caused by the continuous movement of chefs.

With staff on high rotation, NSW is one of the hardest markets to cover. Even the Victorian guide, when I worked on it, had less turnover, and those who've worked overseas tell me Australian chefs and waiters are more mobile than most. One year we had sent the book to press and I was on a break interstate when changes at the Restaurant of the Year meant we had to modify seven pages of the book and find a new winner. We had two hours in which to do it.

While losing a hat was a big deal for most restaurants, I seldom heard from them. Most never rang me asking why they'd been scored lower than the previous year, or wrote to argue their case. We knew they cared because they'd slag us off to our friends (often their customers) and other spies. But precious few actually asked us why we'd made our decisions. And we would always offer reasons when asked. Part of the point we made by standing up in front of these chefs at the awards ceremony was to demonstrate our conviction in our decisions. We would back them up if necessary. In my view a restaurant that didn't ask was a restaurant that either didn't care, or didn't want to be seen as caring. Yet they all cared about hats.

Downgrading wasn't easy. And while it made headlines and made people talk, we didn't do things for effect. In my time there were no bonuses or royalties for selling more books, no benefit to the editors from the old maxim 'any publicity is good publicity'. We called it how we saw it, and we were paid the same whether there were ten three-hat restaurants or two. Taking the decision to remove chef's hats was always a long, drawn-out and difficult decision. But in a country that continues to spout on about how we've the best produce in the world, some things made it easier.

One restaurant we took a hat off had a $65 entree that tasted mainly of butter. At the same restaurant they had white truffles, which, when they're good, are the closest thing I've ever eaten to the perfect flavour. But sadly these were served six months out of season so they had the texture, and arguably the taste, of bleached dog turds. Only a few months previously, in the height of the season, I'd been eating them in Italy, picking chunks up off the table after they were shaved in abandon at a local trattoria. There was no comparison.

Most of the time I was responsible only for myself and my words. But as a *Guide* editor I also saw my role as overseer. All the scores were my responsibility. In addition to the newspaper dining, I trudged my way through suburban Italian restaurants as well as high-flyers. In the first few months after I became the chief reviewer I ate in well over a quarter of the places in the *Guide* that I'd not dined at before. All the while auditing not just the restaurants, but also the reviewers. I made spot checks on our reviewing team by comparing my scores with theirs.

Thankfully, this responsibility was not mine alone. For the entire time that I edited *The Good Food Guide* I was blessed with excellent co-editors; Lisa Hudson for three years, then Simon Thomsen for two. While I was the main reviewer, scouring the city, dining constantly and writing like a demon, I had backup in the form of great editorial expertise. There was no major decision that the two of us didn't agree on.

Where the newspaper score was decided by me and me alone, with no consultation, the giving and taking of hats was more inclusive. Our reviewers were asked for their feedback on any restaurant they thought worthy. Both editors dined their way across the top eateries and we rarely thought differently from each other about the experiences, often months apart. If a restaurant went down in hats we both steadfastly agreed on the course of action. Ditto if they went up. While the newspaper review is a snapshot of a restaurant in time, the book was considered over a longer period. *The Good Food Guide* is more considered, and more consultative.

To ensure a level playing field I put in place certain rules to avoid conflicts of interest. I wouldn't meet with restaurateurs to talk about reviews or offer them advice other than general comments. To do so, or to appear at industry-sponsored events offering advice, would be to step from the role of reviewer to consultant, a fine line but an important distinction.

The book, it must be said, was far more conservative than the newspaper. I could lash a restaurant in print on a Tuesday because it was sloppily run and should be so much better, but if they were good enough for *The Good Food Guide*, the entries had to stand up for a year. A mere 160 words in the book had to point out the positives rather than nitpicking the negatives. Reviews in the *Guide* had to give you a reason to go, rather than ten reasons not to go. We made multiple visits to high-ranking restaurants over a period of months, always with an eye to consistency; the hardest of all things to master. We forgave minor slips or seemingly one-off bad nights. We visited when restaurants were most likely to shine, pored over wine lists, all the time looking at the way they'd thought things through. As editors we tried to see if there was vision in the menu, or just profit; inspiration or just misplaced efforts to make things complicated. And whether they were about credibility or just cash flow.

If we erred it was usually on the side of caution. I inherited the book and its scores, and I passed it on to my successors, who made only minor adjustments in their first year. The book is bigger than any of its editors. If I have any regrets about my time reviewing, it's not about making too many criticisms. It's about having to be nice too often, and having lawyers who are too cautious.

One question that inevitably came up every year after the launch was how we chose the restaurants to review for the book. It was an arduous process – but thorough. First we compiled a long short list of potential reviews. This was based on the previous year's guide, reader recommendations, reviewer recommendations and suggestions from other chefs or foodies. We also considered any restaurant that contacted us hoping to be reviewed. To review a place, first we had to know it existed. A budding restaurant was well served by a phone call, a letter, an email giving contact details, a menu and a convincing argument for us to visit.

The size of the *Guide* is a limiting factor, though – there are a set number of pages, and we would only include the highest scoring restaurants, the kind we would be happy to recommend to friends. Cheap places, particularly Asian restaurants where the food is decent but the other aspects completely lacking, would overfill the book. While giving readers a discerning opinion, we also wanted to promote excellence.

For the newspaper, the reviews followed similar guidelines. I always tried to mix things up week by week, everything from the styles (for example, cuisine, views) to the location and the ranking. A slew of 12-out-of-20 restaurants starts to wear thin, but you can't just invent a higher or lower score. Generally I'd end up with a combination of new places and restaurants in various parts of the city that deserved a review, and hope that the scores offered enough variation to keep everyone happy. Mostly, though, the restaurants that make the paper are new. They're the ones the punters want to know about before they shell out their cash and the restaurateurs are usually gagging for it, too. Anything to help kick-start the business. They hope.

I worked just about every day, often up writing at six am, and getting home at gone eleven pm. They were long days, often made uncomfortable by the extraordinary richness of the food. I'd regularly go to bed feeling completely stuffed, which left me feeling ill the next day, often after a night of sweats, discomfort, and dehydration.

That's the rub. If you want to be a restaurant reviewer, you'd better love food. Lots of it. You don't have an enormous choice about what you eat or when you eat it. Dessert? Sorry, no choice, you have to have one. Coffee? If it gives an insight into the place, then yes. Wine? Well, go on then, twist my arm, and I'll suss out the sommelier while I'm at it.

You can get too much of a good thing. Even though I was in the throes of a love affair with restaurants, and I do have a relatively iron stomach, I often wished I could spread the great meals out over a decade or two, rather than eating at five of Australia's best restaurants in one week. A ten-course lunch might be followed by a twelve-course dinner. There might be two dinners in one night when the schedule was too full, perhaps fifteen lunches and dinners in six days when travelling. It was eating at its most Olympian.

At night after marathon dinners I'd lie awake feeling like a stuffed goose, my heart pounding as I struggled to digest fatty, flavoursome, fantastic meals. My doctor told me to keep my cholesterol in check after only a few months in the job. And what, quit?

I started out as a reasonably thin man of 194 centimetres. Despite daily exercise, I started to expand around the middle, putting on sixteen kilograms in a little over a year. I was never able to wear the strides I'd bought a week prior to starting the gig. My skin became greasy and spotty, my face had a sickly puce tinge, and I continued to put on weight. Being taught to eat everything on my plate as a boy did me no favours in those years. It may be good during times of famine or rationing, but it sure as hell hurt me trying to digest innumerable rich meals a week. Luckily, I usually had help to eat them.

Finding willing reviewers was never much trouble, as you'd expect. (At least one unscrupulous company pretends to be *The Good Food Guide* each year, asking 'reviewers' to pay an annual fee for the privilege.) People offered their services with nagging regularity. If their CV showed some potential, I might suggest they write a sample review even when we didn't need more reviewers at that time. Virtually nobody did. The idea of writing a review was more attractive than actually doing it. And that's the trick.

Dining out can be demanding. Ask any of my ex-girlfriends. There are times when you're sick, tired, not very hungry or too hungry, or not in the mood for Thai, and yet you still have to dine. You don't just swan about in restaurants. You have to be aware of what's going on: as you book, when you arrive and during the meal. Then you have to record it all. Reviewers are paid to notice things. We can't help trying to listen as the couple on table 28 complain to each other about the food or the waiter. We watch over our dining companion's shoulder as a waiter serves a table of six. We're at work when others are out. Sure, we can enjoy ourselves – and whoever hasn't enjoyed themselves at work needs to look for a new job – but a professional reviewer is working every time they eat out. Loving restaurants is one thing, loving going out to dodgy restaurants and trying to find nice things to say about them is another. Reviewers get the good, but they really earn their money going to the bad.

The reviewers I wanted to use for *The Good Food Guide* weren't those that were desperate for a free lunch. People who didn't spend their own money and time in restaurants weren't the people who were useful. The best reviewers are those who are out and about all year, not just during the 'feeding season' – the reviewing period for the *Guide*. While it varies a bit, the feeding is mostly done in autumn, though as the chief reviewer, my responsibility was year-long. All year I'd make regular check-ups on noted restaurants, visit new places for the paper, and make exploratory visits to the least likely of eateries in the hope of making a discovery of some kind. Often it was just more dross in a dreary suburb where, God willing, I didn't leave anything behind so I'd never ever have to go there again.

Being a reviewer comes with responsibility. We had a team of twenty-five people or so, covering the whole of NSW, an area that makes France look small. Specialists in a cuisine or a region knew their patch intimately; others were given widespread restaurants, relating to their skills, their motivation and their interests. Luckily there was a core band of rabid foodies who were willing to take a punt on new restaurants, to drive to all corners of the city and state to see if a restaurant was worthy of inclusion. We wanted people who just adored dining out and looked for excitement, flavour and perfection. And all for little compensation.

Despite the fact they were mostly professionals (cookbook authors, ex-hospitality industry types, food writers and so on), we had pages of notes for our team, covering the how, the why, the what to do and not to do. But occasionally, as with any team, things came unstuck. Arguments erupted at some eateries over what appeared to be trifling matters. Restaurateurs would complain to us about particular visits by reviewers, concerned they may be hard done by. It happened rarely, but it did happen, and while it was our handpicked mob, we didn't take sides. If there were intimations of personal bias we would organise a second visit from a different reviewer. If the suggestion of personal bias was aimed at the editors (and oh, how the restaurants loved to use that as an excuse), we sent other reviewers in our place. We revisited restaurants that we suspected had been an aberration or had a one-off bad night. We made numerous repeat visits to hatted restaurants to be sure of their consistency. We sent unrecognised reviewers to restaurants where the service was said to alter depending on who you were. We asked our team never to book under their own names, to always pay the bill in full, to be discreet, never to divulge scores.

We didn't pay well. Our fees started at $25 a restaurant (plus strictly budgeted expenses), which was hardly good money considering the time and effort, but mostly our reviewers responded with good copy and invaluable insights.

The team was dedicated and talented, but not without hiccups. We had an incident of plagiarism. Some people couldn't convey the sense of a restaurant in the regulation 160 words, taking 350 words to describe pappadums. Others big-noted themselves in restaurants. Instead of being invisible and anonymous they wanted attention. Before my time, reviewers were sometimes restaurateurs; the son of the owner of the first restaurant that I worked in wrote for a national guide. Reviewers in the past had been shagging chefs. We even had an incident where a reviewer disclosed to a restaurant that they'd won a chef's hat award, before any such thing was decided.

Each year, *The Good Food Guide* launch, which is the annual public announcement of the hats, coincided with a kick-arse party for the industry. I'd been as a chef, I'd been as a reviewer and for five years I went as the editor. This party, paid for by a coffee company, had a massive attendance rate. An ocean of champagne was consumed. Chefs dressed up in their finest, or at least their best jeans. Hospitality workers who didn't get an invite tried to gatecrash it. It was an industry night of celebration, even though a handful of restaurateurs wouldn't have something to celebrate. Despite the fact that only award winners were invited – after all, it was a night of winners not losers – some restaurants, those who'd slipped down a rung, weren't happy.

Compiling the book was a huge task, involving many thousands of dollars in meals and lengthy analysis. It may seem arbitrary, but when you eat at every three-hat contender into the space of two weeks, it's easy to compare standards; you can readily rank them from best to worst of the best. And while getting hats can be a good thing for some restaurants, it's amazing how many, in my view naïvely, want three hats.

Even if it is the ultimate accolade, gaining three hats – a world-class ranking during my editorship – is just asking for criticism. It's asking for an endless supply of customers who are looking for faults, and a stream of industry people who will pedantically pick over every word muttered, every ingredient on the plate.

One hat is a great marketing tool. Two seems to let you (sadly) charge pretty steep prices, but three is scary territory. There's only one way to go from there, and it's harder to keep hats than gain them, according to chefs I've spoken to. Again, it's all about consistency. No matter, though; hats are where the action is in terms of Sydney chefs and a lot of Sydney diners too. And three-hat restaurants inevitably get more publicity, and more prestige, even if they're not the best eateries for most people, most of the time.

As part of the *Guide* launch party, we'd employ a host, someone well known as a comedian, who earnt in two hours about two-thirds of what the editor earnt in a year.

The awards party tradition dictated that the editors of the *Guide* stand up in front of all the chefs to present some awards, thank their team, and be in the firing line of all the aggro chefs and restaurants who reckon they've been robbed. I was always reluctant; if you reviewed washing machines or toasters you wouldn't have to do that. And in many ways this was worse. It was their night to show off, to catch up with others in the industry, to celebrate, and here I was, the bloke you'd be as excited to see as the doctor who checked your prostate. I was their antagonist, and here I was standing up in front of them to award hats. It seemed perverse, on the night they should be celebrating, that their adversary should be hogging the limelight. And the onus was on me to get it right. If you looked too chirpy, you didn't see the gravitas in the decisions. If you were too sombre, it could feel like a wake. I've never relished the spotlight, and never less so than on *Good Food Guide* award nights.

For weeks before the launch of my first *Guide* as editor, I was edgy. A big call had seen the former *Guide*'s Restaurant of the Year downgraded to two hats from three. I lost sleep over many of the decisions and my nerves were frayed. When I heard glass smashing at 2 am the night before the launch, I awoke with a start from a dream that involved a torture chamber and every chef I'd ever worked with plus every one I'd met or written about. A junkie had tried to break into the house, blood was dripping down the bars on one of the windows, and I spent the rest of the night awake talking to plod, cleaning up, and generally nervy. By the time the awards came up the next evening, I was emotionally and physically drawn.

That first launch went off well, despite some sound problems. I stuttered my way through a prepared speech and there was a lot more love in the room than I expected, though that could be because we had a lot more winners than the previous year.

Not everyone was happy, of course, the most notable being Banc restaurant, which dropped from three hats to two. As far as we were concerned it was still one of the elite restaurants in one of the world's finest dining cities. It's just that the food wasn't very exciting, they had been rude to me before they realised I was a reviewer (and nauseatingly obsequious after), and multiple visits left several reviewers pondering their elite status. As their name was announced among the two-hat winners, the room went deathly silent and a glass smashed. The chef swore, as chefs are wont to do, and threw his mobile phone into Sydney Harbour.

The worst launch as editor was also my last. As always we'd gone to great lengths to keep the book details secret. We insisted that even the major sponsor couldn't know the results before the night. We'd let only a couple of books out of the publisher's warehouse — to help compile a whiz-bang liftout in the newspaper. But on the Saturday before the Monday launch, the worst happened.

Despite an embargo, *The Good Food Guide* was sold at a suburban bookstore and restaurateurs all over town had a copy even though I still hadn't sighted the finished book. The whole launch night, which hinged on the excitement of the awards announcements, lost its lustre. I was gutted. Not because those responsible never apologised to me. While that irked me then as now, I was angry and annoyed that the industry's biggest party had been spoilt. As several chefs said to me on the night, it's not as much fun when they know the results. It didn't make any difference to me; I knew who had gained and lost hats months before, but that it spoilt the night for the winners was saddening and maddening.

13

Under review

IF I HAVE BEEN hard on chefs, knowing that they're some-times dodgy dealers, then I was and still am twice as critical of restaurant critics. At least chefs work for a living. Most reviewers don't take it seriously enough. To be fair, most don't get paid enough to make it their profession, but a few ethics wouldn't go astray.

A chef can let down a dining room full of people. A restaurant reviewer who is too indolent to visit another restaurant when the one they have just been to isn't really worth reviewing lets down their entire readership. A restaurant is reviewed just once in a blue moon. A regular reviewer is on show each and every week. I knew that if anybody was liable to be accused of incompetence, it was me. What's the old saying – if you can, do; if you can't do, teach; and if you can't teach, criticise?

With that in mind I never reviewed a restaurant in the first week it opened. I think it's lazy and smacks of desperation. Who in their first week in a new job hasn't been able to find the stationery cupboard or work the computer system? Just because staff can seem a little lost, or the food a bit slow, doesn't mean a week later most of the teething problems will still be there. Should the restaurant charge less for that week? Probably. But by the time a review appears in the paper – at best usually a week after the reviewer's visit, plus another week or two before the reader decides they want to go to that restaurant – the place could have improved substantially.

The responsibility of the reviewer is to do the right thing by the reading public. If the chef changes after your meal but before the review is published, you must revisit. If the place is getting substantially better or worse with each meal, then revisit. The most trips I made to one restaurant was six, half at my own expense. Each time I found that the standards had increased, a series of incremental improvements meaning the place, est., earnt an extremely rare but well deserved 18 out of 20.

I get angry at lazy restaurants but lazy reviewers are far worse. They have more readers than the restaurants have diners, more responsibility and none of the pressure of a dining room or kitchen. Reviewers who don't revisit when there is just cause let down everybody – their readers, the diners and their publications. And sadly, lazy reviewing has long been the norm in this country.

I don't think most reviewers know what they're doing. I recently read a review in the national press of a French restaurant. The reviewer said that the braised beef was 'overcooked and nowhere near as tender as it should be.' Hello? Does the reviewer, someone who holds the trust of the public in their hand, actually know the process of meat cookery, the way protein reacts to heat? Braised meat is cooked in liquid, à la stew. If it's tough, it's not cooked enough. It's certainly not overcooked. This reviewer goes on to say that meat in French restaurants is usually 'under' cooked. No, if that's the way meat is usually served in French restaurants, it isn't undercooked, it's cooked *right* (perhaps *bleu*, rare or still mooing would be more constructive and descriptive terms). Maybe it's less cooked than the reviewer likes (the French do love their steaks very bloody), but not 'undercooked'. Small points, yes, but hardly the stuff you need to be a chef to know, and poor knowledge and understanding suggests poor judgement.

Writing like this makes reviewers look like fools. I know I made my fair share of mistakes, but I hope things you'd learn in a high school cooking class aren't among them. Reviewers have a great gig, and they should show enough respect to their employers, the restaurants and their readers to either learn a few things before going out to eat, or at least by doing some research afterwards.

There are different types of reviewers just as there are diners, from the naïve and easily impressed to the discerning. There are those who just use the column to entertain rather than inform, and those who just inform without entertaining, and both probably have a place. There's also another sort altogether. The Restaurant and Catering Association knows that about 16 per cent of the population are what's called 'reluctants', people who really don't want to eat out, and won't enjoy it, regardless of how fault-less the experience is. These reluctant diners can't believe food, something they can attempt at home, costs them money. They're the angry, unplacatable eater. Remarkably, some of them become reviewers. These restaurant critics want to find fault. They want to pick on things. They want to visit in the first week because it makes the restaurant look bad and them look good; it gives them the excuse to write some excitingly critical copy.

It's important to try and stay impartial, to stay excited and to not dominate every single review written in the town. Plurality of voices is better for everyone. When I was in the hot seat I wouldn't review for another publication that offered the equivalent of chef's hats. I wouldn't write feature stories about stand-alone NSW restaurants because it smacks of favouritism and bias. I don't respect reviewers who exercise too much power or greed.

I don't think the dining public should have to put up with reviews that say things like 'there's a new chef starting next month'. Such reviews are essentially meaningless as far as the food is concerned. I also have no respect for mindless comments such as 'my partner declared the dish satisfactory', as if the reviewer hadn't, wouldn't, or couldn't try it themselves and offer an opinion. It makes me mad. Madder than a Swiss hotel chef after a bad review. Madder than a drug-addled, overworked, publicity-driven chef when the power goes off as they appear on the small screen. Really, really mad.

I did visit some restaurants in the first week, but as the first of multiple visits. Sometimes you'd feel like royalty, given the excited attention of the waiting staff and the smell of fresh paint permeating the air at every table. The important thing isn't how a restaurant opens, but how they continue, so if they open poorly, and remain poor a couple of weeks later, you can see the level they will probably attain. If they open well, then drop in standard, that's an indication of the future. Most, however, open with dramas (ever worked with a builder and deadlines?) and get better from there. A discerning reader who is an actual diner doesn't care about the first-night nerves as much as they care about what standard of food and service they'll get when they arrive.

In some cities, such as London, reviewers almost race each other to be the first to write about a restaurant. I've heard of one critic visiting a restaurant for a pre-opening dinner just so they could be first into print. Being first, in some places, is more important than being accurate. And in some of the world's biggest cities, being funny or cruel or first is the whole aim of the restaurant review. Actual responsibility for your review comes second to readership and circulation.

Some reviewers for other publications judge a restaurant by taking points off for perceived mistakes. I reckon these reviewers don't look for the true pleasure in what's out there. 'Oh golly gosh, I can't hear my companions. That's one point off.'

'That waiter has a nose ring, deduct another point.'

'This sauce is technically perfect, no points off.'

My view is that this kind of reviewing is old school and lets down a country on the ascendant. Being technically accurate, or delivering the menu in two minutes rather than three, doesn't make for perfection. And it sure as hell doesn't equal excitement. This kind of reviewing will always favour the status quo, because it doesn't reward successful innovation. Some of the most highly rated chefs in the world, including those with three Michelin stars in multiple restaurants, run the most competent, consistent, reliable restaurants I've ever been to. But the food, I have to say, is boring. Adept, probably textbook renditions yes, but not all that exciting. Service can be polished, but robotic. Other chefs, all around the world, produce extraordinary, exhilarating food, delivered by waiters with personality. Under the system I used, they'd get points for excitement, for magic, for integrity and for daring to go where no-one has gone before – and doing it with breathtakingly good flavours. Groundbreaking does have its risks, but calculated risks with talented chefs are those a youthful nation should consider taking.

There's another type of reviewer, the one who gets to know the chef and is affected by that knowledge or relationship. You can still see favouritism towards certain chefs, particularly in Sydney, where a chef may be judged by how much charity work they do, or how many committees they sit on or how they work like a demon. But if they don't cook as well as the mean-spirited, insolent psycho who charges the same money, you have to criticise them nonetheless. It's strange, but I had both intense admiration for chefs, and little respect for them at the same time. A kind of 'I like what you can do, but I can't care about you as a person' attitude. Because of my job, I felt that I couldn't become personally involved. And if they thought me an arsehole when I was being honest, so be it.

Many of the nearly 2500 meals I ate during my time at *The Sydney Morning Herald* were self-funded. Some meals were eaten interstate or overseas, virtually all the travel at my own expense. I took myself off to Paris, to the south of France, to fifteen regions of China, to Italy, Vietnam, Denmark, the US, Latvia, and the UK for work.

I'd try to make the most of my money, catching a train

and bus to England's famed out-of-London restaurant The Fat Duck (and having to walk to another village to get back after I missed the afternoon bus home). I combined my annual holiday with research, comparing Australia's most international city with the rest of the country and the rest of the world. And I took my responsibility seriously. If you are going to write about food, you must *know* about food.

Judging the judges is paramount if we want good, honest restaurant critiques. I assess reviewers by a few criteria. If they say a place is too loud, or too dark, they're too old. If they go out angrily and unnecessarily looking for faults, they're faulty. If they don't keep the discerning diner in mind, they may be a good read, but not a reliable witness.

A good reviewer:

- Books under an assumed name and always pays for their meal.
- Reviews a restaurant at its most typical. Sunday night, for most restaurants, is not typical.
- Revisits if they don't think they got a complete picture of the place.
- Criticises and praises in equal measure (though not in equal measure for each restaurant, only as they deserve it).
- Tells you more about the place you'll eat at than their dining companions or their funny anecdotes. This is more important in places where there is a paucity of seriously critical reviews.
- Never reviews a restaurant they know will a) be closed, b) be renovated, or c) change chef shortly

after the review is published. I call this the 'what's the point?' principle.

- Knows a lot about food, but doesn't assume too much reader knowledge in the review. Reviewers who don't know how a daube differs from a stew are not just slack, but also incompetent.
- Puts the reader first.
- Isn't mates with a chef that he or she reviews.
- Isn't afraid of chefs, restaurateurs, or law suits.
- Calls a shocker a shocker.
- Writes descriptively so even if they hate it you may think you'll like it, and vice versa.
- Is obvious with their biases.
- Doesn't judge a restaurant based on its customers.
- Has eaten a lot of cuisines, in a lot of countries.
- Makes you hungry for good restaurants and empowers you to cope with the duds.
- Doesn't try to defend restaurants against other reviewers' points of view. That's the restaurants' job.
- Names the chef, to make them accountable.
- Doesn't brag about celebrities who dine at the restaur-ant. Fame doesn't buy taste. Insecure review-ers use this as a trick to back their opinions and make themselves look good.

There's an endless fascination with restaurant reviewing. Everybody eats, everybody has some opinion and the general opinion on reviewers is that we've the best job in the world and we're on the take. Jay Rayner, a reviewer for the *Observer* in the UK, points out that you can be a war correspondent or a serious journalist dealing with important topics such as child abuse and only get a polite letter perhaps every few months — and yet the feedback for frivolous writing, about restaurants no less, generates relatively enormous response.

From the start I was fully aware of people actually reading the reviews. It wasn't like my weekly recipe column, where for years I thought only my mother read it (until I stuffed up by not putting in an ingredient and was accused of hitting the cooking sherry by a couple of correspondents). A debate started in the press about my second review when I said a $7 coffee was expensive. I knew there were even more expensive coffees out there, but the topic hit a note. Funny thing though, I also found that reviewers are talked about even more than they're talked to, especially when they first start out. Restaurateurs bitched, readers talked, your friends would have an opinion, but often there was silence unless you rang or emailed someone, or stepped into a restaurant or café.

The biggest change for me was probably in the response from people I'd meet. Suddenly I became of interest at parties. People wanted to know what it was like to eat out, HOW GOOD is the job, and what was my favourite restaurant. The topic of my work, which I'd have been as excited about had it been reviews of IT gadgetry or regional theatre troupes, tended to dominate conversation. I had always been obsessed and passionate about food, but that was just what I was into. Yet since food in Australia means fashion, and the reviews were so widely read, I found I was thrust into a new realm of conspicuousness. Girls invited me to come over and 'bring your best pyjamas.' I had others call and say they wanted to fuck my brains out. For a bloke not interested in power, not driven by ambition, not desiring of fame, and a long way from being wealthy or a rock star, it came as something of a shock.

At the same time, however, I became used to a certain sound when people met me. They emitted an involuntary kind of 'aouwhh' noise, the tone dropping at the end in an expression of disappointment. I don't know what they expected but I was happy being me: a dag who looked crumpled and uncomfortable in just about any get-up, just another dickhett being given an outlet for his opinion. People who met me must have expected something a little better. I wasn't interesting. I wasn't awe-inspiring. I wasn't controversial or colourful or sexy or even close to neat. I wasn't wealthy or morbidly obese or cantankerous. I was just Australia's worst dressed reviewer, an ordinary bloke with an extraordinary job.

14

Are you free tonight?

'YOU'RE NOT reviewing restaurants,' my sister said categorically one day. 'You're reviewing women.'

At the time I'd only been living in Melbourne for a couple of months and I'd moved knowing just a single person who I could ask out for dinner. I was busy reviewing about twenty-five restaurants in town and the same number in the country. I could, at a real pinch, have eaten at them alone, but I'd have to order four or five courses at every meal, and bugger it, I was new to the city, so anybody who didn't have two heads and could conduct part of a conversation was invited out to dinner. 'I'm the tall one who used to be skinny,' I'd offer as a description when I had to meet up with someone I didn't already know. It seemed better than carrying a rose between my teeth. Despite indications to the contrary, however, I just needed dinner dates, not an endless supply of lovers. Considering my experience with women, I was far better qualified to review restaurants.

But okay, yes, a whole bunch of mostly single females did become my dining companions. Honestly, it was for work. Women are more interested in food than most men, and the single ones are usually available at short notice. That's all.

The problem arose when the invitation was misconstrued. I should've realised. It happened once when the words 'my boyfriend is very open-minded,' were whispered in my ear. We'd just laughed ourselves silly after watching a rat meander under tables at a bad Italian restaurant in Sydney, when I was still in my critical youth. It still happened years later, when my lover was interstate and I took another woman to dinner who looked crestfallen when I spoke of my sweetheart and how much I adored her. I'd presumed she knew I was attached. I'm sure there are a few gay friends who weren't sure about their dinner invitations, either, and whether they should ask me back for 'coffee'. I'll make it clear now, it's what's above the table-cloth that counts, at least to this food anorak.

To be sure, dining out is an incredibly sexy way to spend an evening, but take it from someone who has observed the machinations in more dining rooms than he cares to think of: while it's fantastically romantic if you already know each other, one-on-one dining is hardly the most relaxed way to meet a lover.

Dating, the American style of inviting a relative stranger to dinner in the hope of finding a soulmate, sucks. Going out for dinner in a swank restaurant is a stupid way to get to know someone. I watched it all the time: the awkwardness, the difficult conversation, the way the chemistry — more often than not — suddenly proved unworkable, before the menu had even arrived. I have watched waiters trying to speed up meals for diners who were so on edge they looked like they'd been given a death sentence, some squirming while they planned their escape, others pale with the realisation of the amount they were spending on a pretty dire night out. I always hoped that, at the very least, they enjoyed the food.

Reviewing may have been a form of paid dating for me, but I'm not your usual diner. Food has some extra relevance to me above and beyond the company I'm in. It's a flaw that I've been lucky enough to exploit for my work, a capacity to see the restaurant and their tucker irrespective of personal happiness.

The signs were there well before I started reviewing. I was once dining at a flash restaurant near the water, the kind of place that sold two lamb shanks for $33 in the early 1990s. In front of me was my girlfriend of some time, all dolled up, but plainly on edge, a woman about to break up with me. Yep, you guessed it, Lynn again. She was sobbing inconsolably. I looked at her across the double-clothed table, taking in her utter devastation, her chest shaking, her eyes flooded with tears, her cheeks flushed and wet with grief.

And my thoughts? 'Oh my God, she intends to leave me. Again. She's so gorgeous, I wish I could rewind five minutes. I wish I could make everything all right. I'm going to be utterly heartbroken. Doesn't that saffron work amazingly well with the mash and hapuka fillet? How can I undo what's been done, unsay what's been said? I'll be crushed if this is the end of our life together. Where do they get such amazingly ripe tomato from? I wonder what's for dessert. Oh, she's still crying.'

It's shallow, I know. It's just that food resonates with me. I can still taste her tears all these years later, but I can also remember that particular dish, a combination of textures and flavours that will forever linger in my memory, and, yes, always remind me of her.

That failing, that quirk in my personality, was a godsend when I started reviewing. I found I was able to dispassionately judge a restaurant regardless of the company I was in or how the night was going. Separating personal from professional life, I now realise, was the way I'd been taught. Don't get a life, Fritz the Old German Bastard had told me in my teens. Don't bring your personal problems to work. Never has the capacity to separate the two been more useful than as the chief reviewer for *The Sydney Morning Herald*. It gave me some ability to see a restaurant through the fresh, innocent eyes of a stranger – though I don't think it's done me any favours on a personal level. I was often too involved with the eating to notice the advances being made, or the insults being dealt out.

If I was reviewing and having a bad night, I had to ensure the restaurant didn't wear it. I had many bad nights out personally at great restaurants. To me, that's the responsibility of a public palate: to judge a restaurant on its ability to affect people who are in the right frame of mind. It's not the restaurants' fault some people are cranky when they arrive, or fight with the hubby before the entrees even hit the table.

Being able to differentiate between what a restaurant offers and what I was experiencing in my life became an art. It allowed me to score restaurants highly that I probably wouldn't choose to visit more than once. I became the sponge, the restaurant tofu, taking up the flavour of each eatery rather than contributing to it, the passive reviewer who flitted from place to place, rarely having time or the freedom to revisit for social occasions, but enjoying each place for what it was.

The ability to enjoy restaurants regardless of storms in my life became my saviour when I moved out of my house while it was renovated. I was writing major reviews and visiting the state's best restaurants, but it was also my darkest hour. I lived in a garage for a few months. For a time I had no kitchen in which to test my weekly recipe column, no office in which to write or edit *The Good Food Guide*. My latest relationship was falling apart, and a film crew had me on edge as they followed seemingly every move for a documentary about the *Guide*. But, luckily, I could still see the good in restaurants.

The night of clarity came when a girl left me sitting idly in a very swank modern Greek restaurant for over an hour. Staff quietly removed her cutlery, brought a solo menu and kept a discreet distance, seeing my pain. Yet I still scored the restaurant a rare 16 out of 20 and gave it two hats in *The Good Food Guide*.

It worked both ways. I celebrated winning a major court case by blowing nearly $1000 at a three-hat restaurant that left me strangely cold. We drank well, the mood was upbeat, but I was markedly underwhelmed by the food. My worst six months of restaurant reviewing coincided with falling in love. I was buoyed by a newfound intimacy, where each meal was a rediscovery of myself, but the restaurants were often complete duds. A great mood was tested by far too many slipshod restaurants, too many try-hard chefs and waiters whose attitude stank.

The matter of who to dine out with was important to me, but not for the usual reasons people choose dinner dates. Despite my sister's assertion, I didn't want a parade of new faces in front of me each evening; instead I craved stability. I wanted to do my job, and that involved concentrating on the décor, the food and the mood, not the low-cut dress in front of me or the hand in my lap. And I didn't want to have to say 'just a moment' as a new date made herself more comfortable, while I wrote notes about the meal, the room, the service, in the hour following dinner.

There were rules. No telling anyone where we're going. No cleavage (hey, a bloke's got to concentrate). I'll pay. I'll choose. Ask the waiter any menu questions, not me. Let me face the room. Don't use the words 'reviewer' 'Good Living' 'Good Food Guide' or my full name. Don't brag to the waiter that we're reviewing (this happened more than once, seriously, and I wanted to crawl in a hole and die).

My dining companions were often other reviewers. A few were former industry people – a sommelier, a chef, a waiter – who'd left hospitality as I had, but retained their passion for restaurants. A few were lawyers who had become friends. Yes, it is possible. Occasionally my companions were family, the same people who had subsidised my dining when I first started reviewing.

All were hungry souls, happy to keep our dining destinations secret until after we'd visited, taking calls of confirmation on my behalf and giving me feedback on the way they were treated. 'Like a private investigator,' one flatmate described the experience of reconfirming bookings in several names and the clandestine visits.

My companions could tell anyone who asked what they thought of the meal, but not what I thought. They had to order what I wanted them to order, and hand over their plate so I could try their food.

They had to sit and look at the wall while I always got a view of the room. They understood if I looked at them kind of vacantly, as I made the most of the peripheral vision I have been lucky enough to be born with. Some of them I trusted to take in details, to watch for me, to record things like timing, décor, the waiters' movements and attitude when I couldn't see them. Others might know more about a particular type of cuisine or style of cooking. Mostly, they were pliable so the night ran the way I wanted it to. It was my place of work, after all.

My friends and my partner throughout much of that time were my saviours. They understood if I suddenly became distracted by the conversation on table 43 or asked what seemed to be stupid questions. They covered for me when the waiters asked 'did you enjoy that,' because – legally – I couldn't really say I liked it to save their feelings and then say I hated it in print.

Women who thought that I had the best job in the world, and lusted at the thought of dining out (even if it was with me) were surprised at how quickly the lustre wore off. Virtually all of them said that they loved eating out, only to pull the plug a few days later saying 'can we stay in tonight,' or 'can we just have one course,' or 'I don't feel like going out.' Reviewers always feel like going out.

It wasn't that safe dining out with me, either. At a flash Melbourne restaurant, Pomme, my girlfriend of the time jerked her head suddenly and was collected on the noggin by one of those enormous white plates as the waiter attempted to put it down. Her eyes filled with tears, a bruise shone crimson on her forehead and she disappeared to the loo for a while. A long while. When she eventually reappeared, all prettied up but with red-rimmed eyes, she sported a golf ball–sized embolism that stuck out from under her fringe. But we stayed on for dinner, because, well, we wanted to. Well, I know I wanted to.

While one-on-one dining may not be ideal for initial dates, reviewing did allow me the privilege of taking out one person at a time. Most reviews weren't done in a group – I found the conversation too distracting, the dishes too many, and I ate too little of them to be sure of their worth. Sometimes one person in the group would forget what we were there for and gobble all theirs down before I had a chance to taste it. Others ordered the same thing as someone else, a worthless meal for a reviewer. And most of the time the expenses budget only covered a meal for two.

By contrast, taking one person at a time allowed me to build deeper friendships. Instead of merely relating to couples, I'd get to know one partner at a time. I bonded with people in a far deeper sense by being thrust together with them for three hours. Without the inference of sexual pressure women became even more fascinating. And alluring. I'd argue that it's true that a woman who shows an interest in food is a woman with other hearty, primal appetites.

Dinner discussions were mostly about things other than food or restaurants – a rule that helped avoid private conversations being overheard by waiters, and a way for me to stay sane in a world dominated by those topics. I heard about other people's passions, be it film, native bush, symphony, indie bands, swingers' clubs, the law, art, anything other than my work. What's more, it was usually done over a glass of something sultry from a bottle.

That's not to say I didn't find a little romance along the way. I met a woman in Melbourne who jumped me after a series of reviews, and we shared several great years together, more often than not socialising over a lunch or dinner out. I've been lucky enough to have had amorous meals paid for by the newspaper, along with dinners where friendships were cemented, and deals done.

I've fallen in love, had my heart broken, sobbed, laughed, had the bottom fall from my world and found my life changed by restaurants. I've been privy to other people meeting, getting engaged, celebrating fiftieth anniversaries, groping and dumping each other. Restaurants are wonderfully exciting places that bear witness to the most amazing moments in people's lives. And they're one hell of a place in which to work.

15

The power of celebrity

ONLY AN IDIOT would choose to be in front of a documentary camera. And there I was. Hundreds of hours of raw footage into the doco that would become *Heat in the Kitchen*, I kept reminding myself that even a saint can look like an arsehole at the hands of a wilful editor. The jokes, the offhand remarks, the tired and emotional moments – cut them all together and I could come out smelling a bit iffy.

It wasn't supposed to be like this. When *The Sydney Morning Herald* agreed to let a documentary crew follow the process of compiling *The Good Food Guide*, my involvement was to be minor. I agreed to do a couple of interviews from which a few short snippets would appear. My face would be pixelated in the interest of me trying to keep a low profile at restaurants. But my co-editor at the time left the job a few months into the reviewing season, and I had to honour our agreement about access. Suddenly I was thrust into a starring role.

The doco crew became a nagging presence in my daily landscape. They were there on reviewing trips to the Hunter Valley, they were in my home, at the office and in the restaurants. Often they'd secretly film me dining out, then interview me afterwards on seedy street corners.

Wine and early starts conspired to make me slightly more incoherent than I'd like to have been on telly, and only enhanced my suet-like pallor under street lights. I spent enough time standing on gritty, urban sidewalks while the crew checked 'levels' to get a good insight into another, older profession at the same time. It was a good distraction from what was plainly a ridiculous circumstance for me. My work required that I try to stay anonymous, but it also required me to swan about (in a guarded, uncomfortable, you're-going-to-misrepresent-me kind of fashion) with a camera crew all day and night.

If you want to see a reluctant face on telly, I'm usually it. My talent for it is roughly proportional with my desire. The first time I did a promo for a book on Italy my mouth went so dry I couldn't speak. I went on New Zealand morning television to talk about judging Auckland restaurants and just about froze. Nightly current affairs shows sometimes asked me to come on to discuss the legalisation of kangaroo meat or the relative merits of frozen vegetables. Mostly I'd decline, as I did when I was asked to try out for the critic's role on *My Restaurant Rules*. At the time I was busy trying to avoid getting even my picture in the paper. I desperately hoped that this doco, scheduled for the public broadcaster SBS, would make a tiny splash and fade away.

As it was, the five-part *Heat in the Kitchen* series was promoted heavily during the high-rating Ashes cricket series, with a snippet from me saying 'the only thing bigger than the Sydney restaurant scene is Sydney chefs' egos'. Later it went onto high rotation on pay TV. As a result, quite a few people saw it. I went from being a relatively invisible restaurant critic with a small modicum of notoriety to a person off the telly. Suddenly I was being accosted in the street on my morning walk. One lunchtime I was quietly reviewing a new restaurant when a customer screamed hysterically across the room, 'I saw you on the telly last night!' The tables were turned. For the rest of the meal all eyes were on me, rather than the other way around.

In another ironic twist, I was now at the mercy of newspaper TV critics. I was, accordingly, 'tartly reticent,' 'uneven' and 'pedestrian talent'. All patently true and quite fair. Bloody critics.

There was no benefit to me financially, professionally or personally in having my dial on the box. But for the chefs who were followed by the documentary crew, it was different. I'm sure they felt equally imposed upon by the relentless presence of cameras in their restaurants and homes, but in advertising terms, it was a small price. Even the Olympian swearing efforts of Restaurant Balzac's Matthew Kemp couldn't put a dent in the phenomenal pulling power of television.

Chefs are relatively new to this cult of celebrity. Sydney created the trend of Australian celebrity chefs in the early 1990s. Food commentators were revering the talent in the kitchen long before most other states realised that food didn't come from a rotund, curly-moustached cliché in a tall hat. Putting the emphasis on the chefs, giving them a profile and a reputation like rock stars, puts the onus on them to keep standards up. Good food, good reputation; bad food, reputation compromised. I made a conscious decision as a food writer to name chefs, and to give them credit where due. If I said the pannacotta trembled like a frightened bird on the plate, then the chef should deliver that each and every time. If it was rubbery, they should take responsibility.

It always seemed odd to me when restaurant reviews didn't mention chefs at all – as if the food had got there by magic. In the bad old days, many restaurant owners didn't even know their chef's full name. I was called Andrew for the first two and a half years of my apprenticeship. But naming chefs in the public sphere gave them ownership, and helped engender pride in one of the hardest jobs there is. It was a small token of recognition for the crap hours, the crap social life, the anger and angst of cooking.

Then came the television chef, affording the kind of profile that geeky apprentices in the 1980s never dreamed of. And there are still plenty of opportunities for the right kind of person. I've fielded countless calls from production companies, PR firms, magazines and television stations looking for gorgeous, vivacious, preferably female talent with cooking ability. Haven't they seen what a lifetime of kitchen work does to your skin, let alone your social skills? Most of the time chefs are poorly socialised, locked away in the back rooms of hotels and restaurants, reluctant to talk to a customer let alone a camera. They have difficulty being civil to the person in human resources, or their dealers, grunting obscenities or inanities to each other. It's hardly a breeding ground for celebrity. Thankfully there are exceptions – those with talent, opportunity and drive. And a certain photogenic appeal, naturally.

At least ten Sydney chefs have had television shows, boosting their profile and doubtless their restaurant bookings. Reality TV cashed in with *My Restaurant Rules*, creating whole new ideas about reality in restaurant land (restaurants are more likely to have wolves at their doors than queues).

Even outside television, celebrity chefs are breeding like white rabbits. People such as Joël Robuchon and Alain Ducasse from France, along with good telly talent such as Gordon Ramsay from the UK, have multiple restaurants in several countries, making money and a bigger name for themselves in the process. Las Vegas and Shanghai are spending huge amounts to snare restaurants from top-notch talent such as the incredible US chef Thomas Keller, and it's just a matter of time before Australian chefs are offered the same. Melbourne's Crown Casino is spending $10 million fitting out a space for the multinational restaurant owner Nobu, and has already welcomed a version of Neil Perry's Rockpool. Soon to come are Sydney's Guillaume at Bennelong and the team from Icebergs. It could be goodbye cottage industry with uniquely good and interesting cooking, hello brand.

With the corporatisation of restaurants come new expectations. Like the 'named' chef being within a thousand kilometres of the stove. Personally I don't think the executive chef needs to be cooking to make the experience great. I've found that some of Sydney's best restaurants can be better when the chef's not cooking. Why? Because the second chef is also talented, and while the telly chef is swanning about doing photo shoots and airline catering, the second has a greater feel for the food. As a bonus, the second can bask in the reflected glory. In the 1990s, at least one three-hat restaurant was widely regarded as being off the boil on Mondays, the day the celebrity chef was actually on the pans and his second on a day off. It's a feel thing. The more you cook, the better you should be at it. The more you're away from the stoves, the harder it becomes to cook well when you're under pressure. And being handy in front of a Handicam doesn't mean everything will run like it does on the telly when you get in front of the stove.

Being great talent for TV means chefs can kick the rest of their career along. The people who come to their restaurants aren't necessarily better eaters, or more discerning; they might just want to see someone famous. But the colour of their money is the same, and celebrity spotting comes with a price tag. For basking in the aura of fame, many will happily pay, even if they're no more likely to get a good meal. It could be that in the kitchen ego has taken over from self-belief, arrogance from steely determination. Diners seeking quality without the bells and whistles can sometimes be left feeling disappointed and considerably less flush. The passionate artisan who shuns publicity is often a better bet.

Celebrity in restaurants is like celebrity everywhere: mindless and of dubious merit. Endorsements by celebrity chefs are big business, but if a chef says an electric wok is good, it isn't necessarily so. Chefs have been paid to promote crap packet pasta, bottled simmer sauces, soap, cheese, and stoves. Some get writing gigs when they can't write, or a recipe book where they get someone else to write the recipes. Of course they have a right to make money from these gigs; as stand-alone businesses, restaurants hardly overload the bank account. If chefs want to sell their credibility to fill supermarket shelves or get their face on the box then good luck to them. But diner beware. When brand overshadows individualism, when formula replaces passion, and when style wins over substance, the magic of great restaurant food starts to unravel.

16

A chopstick through the heart

ANOTHER REVIEWER PASSED on the message from a waiter. 'Tell Matthew I'd like to shove a chopstick through his heart.'

The comment at least assumed I had one. A heart, that is.

When I originally snared the job as chief critic for *The Sydney Morning Herald*, I said I wasn't in the job to make friends. Well, I certainly succeeded at that. There were times, occasionally, when I was showered with affection on a visit to a restaurant, though I was never sure if it was sham or real. The great downside of reviewing, however, was not the good feedback, but the bad. The threats. The cajoling. The mindless emails sent not just by restaurateurs but by their staff or their competitors or mates. I was even hijacked by a colleague at the newspaper I wrote for, a journalist in the news department, who tried to escalate some supposed 'dispute' between myself and former three-hat chef Neil Perry by quoting me out of context. 'Plunged the blade a little deeper,' was the journalist's comment after he cherry-picked a short piece I'd been asked to write, justifying the chef's demotion. Clearly my piece hadn't been adversarial enough.

I know what it's like to be reviewed. I know that if you slog over a dish and someone doesn't like it, it feels like a slap in the face. I knew when I became a restaurant reviewer that I wasn't going to be saying nice things all the time. Week after week I was actually quite kind. In fact I was very positive, forgiving most faults, trying to see the best in a restaurant, only criticising when necessary but looking to be constructive. If you dine out often and don't look for positives, especially in this country, you're going to have an ordinary time, every time.

Hospitality is a fine art, mixing theatre, personalities, improvisation, chemistry, heat, egos and fresh produce. Things often go awry. At least half the responsibility for having a good time falls on the customer. If there's a waiter you hate, why not make a game of trying to get them to smile? If it's the food that lets you down, well, hell, complain, but don't take it personally. Get merry and go home and don't go back.

For me, however, criticising was the point. I was paid to notice the faults. I went out to enjoy myself, but I earnt my money by being discerning and judgemental. While I expected criticism to breed criticism – of me – I wasn't prepared for mindless abuse directed my way. Especially from restaurants I hadn't even written about.

There were many threats before and following reviews. There was a range of menacing 'I'm from Calabria' style communiqués – pointing out a certain intimacy with people in the 'Ndrangheta, the most infamous arm of the Italian mafia that has infiltrated Australia. And more prosaic ones:

'I'll punch your fucking head in if I see you around Darling Harbour.'

'We have 600 years of family history and we'll crush you like an ant.'

'I have friends in high places.'

'What would you know, hanging around with your eastern suburbs mates … don't ever come back or I'll throw you out.'

'I know where you live.'

Not to mention, 'I fear for your safety,' from a restaurant PR.

I probably would have been threatened more often if I didn't try to keep my phone number private. Working from a home office means there's no distinction between work and leisure time. Even then you don't need abusive Sunday phone calls. I get enough of those in my private life. I used the newspaper's switchboard as a contact number, so they'd put through all the calls during office hours. Most of the callers hung up if they got an answering machine. Others went speechless when they spoke to a live reviewer. Others wanted to meet face to face, the suggestion and the tone one of intimidation. I didn't meet with chefs or restaurateurs about reviews; business was kept to the phone. It was a blanket rule: no fear, no favour. Not meeting with restaurateurs meant that I avoided a lot of threats, but also that I avoided bribes. Only once was I directly offered a financial incentive to write a good review and that was from someone so drunk they probably don't even remember making the call.

It was important to stay aloof and have no allegiances. The belief in a so-called food-mafia – an 'in' club that supposedly held sway in Sydney before my time – was not going to have any legs during my tenure. I wouldn't drink with chefs. I wouldn't socialise with them. The easiest option was to maintain a discreet distance. If it came off as arrogance, then so be it. I'd rather seem remote than disingenuous.

To this day I'm still getting veiled threats. Disgruntled, unstable and possibly unhinged restaurateurs can't get over a bad review. They pretend it doesn't matter, then blast you with bile. One of the 'Good Living' editors at *The Sydney Morning Herald* even coined a particularly crude collective noun for chefs, 'That Bunch of Cunts,' after dealing with too many meth-dropping psychos who ran kitchens.

The clever restaurants made the most of any publicity. My favourite response to a review arrived in the form of an advertising campaign run by a restaurant that I had scored 9 out of 20. The publicity material had offered me a free kick, spruiking that 'the food is rooted,' and I couldn't have agreed more, though they continued, 'in Japanese cuisine.'

The first week after the review the restaurant ran an ad in 'Good Living', the same food pages I wrote for. The ad sported hundreds of simple round smiley faces all jostling for space, and one grumpy one, with words to the effect of 'Ten thousand satisfied customers and only one unhappy one.' The next week the ad featured even more smiley faces so the single grumpy one, presumably me, was virtually obscured; the number of satisfied customers had also risen by a few thousand. Eventually the restaurant went out of business but you can't blame me. Blame all those satisfied customers who didn't go back. Or the fact the food was rooted.

Of course, criticism is hard to take. Any home cook knows that. Just try and slate someone's food the next time you go over to their place for dinner and see how they take it. And how often you get invited back. Even restaurants' designers took offence, as only designers can. A reference (which, incidentally, wasn't mine) in *The Good Food Guide* to the carpet in a flash harbourside diner as 'giving ageing hippies flashbacks' was met with a letter from the sensitive soul who'd chosen it, taking exception to our view and suggesting perhaps it was us who were aesthetically challenged.

Restaurants, good and bad, can survive a negative review by giving their customers what they want. The best run restaurant, in a business sense, is one that stays open. At best my reviews were read by under a million people. That leaves about four million people in the greater Sydney area alone that a restaurateur can gouge, even if the critic hates the place. I failed Sydney's most famous restaurant, Doyle's, giving them a well deserved 7 out of 20, variously described in the media as a 'pasting' and a 'sledging' — and they are still trading happily a couple of years down the track.

Despite my rule not to meet with chefs or restaurateurs, I was sometimes thrust among them, especially at the annual *Good Food Guide* awards.

At one of these ceremonies, after a two-year, several thousand dollar deliberation that saw a restaurant downgraded from two hats to one, I was bailed up. Usually I had a mob of friends who kept an eye on me at these events, stepping in when it got ugly. But this night they were having too good a time. An angry man with a head as red as an infected pimple starting putting me straight on just how wrong I'd got it with one restaurant. He ranted and raved, spraying me with verbal toxin. He wasn't just some aggressive partygoer, however, or some passionate diner whose favourite eatery had fallen from grace. He was the silent owner of the restaurant in question. As the (surprisingly more level-headed) chef of the restaurant said to me later, 'Why the fuck did he have to stop being silent tonight?'

The thing about hospitality is its passion. Most in the game aren't in it to make a huge profit – hey, there's better and easier money to be made almost anywhere. Restaurant people do it because they love it. And it's not just the restaurants that are obsessed, it's their customers, too. People take dining out seriously. What surprised me most about reviewing was the angst and bitterness.

A few weeks into the job I gave a high score to a new restaurant. In the same week that I visited it, I'd been to the four other three-hat restaurants, the cream of Sydney's eateries. The best meal was at the newcomer. This place had over ten chefs. It had five different coffees from single origins. It had a wine list that blew your mind. And it had overwrought but mostly quite incredible dishes served in a succession of plates and styles, twenty-two of which I ate at one sitting for a little over $120. It was amazing. But the response to the review shocked me. Readers shook my arm from its socket and thanked me for introducing them to the place. But green-eyed chefs went looking for faults. They tried to undermine me, bitched to my editors, my colleagues. Apparently a positive review could generate more flak than a negative one.

When I wrote about Sean's Panaroma, arguably the most Sydney of eateries and well loved for it, another restaurant crowed that they were happy they didn't get the same (high) score as a 'grubby café'. Now for all the hundreds of people that visit this and other high-profile restaurants each week, some will, undoubtedly, have a bad experience. Maybe the wheels fell off that day. Maybe they got the waiter who had lost his job by the next morning. Maybe they were reluctant diners looking for things to criticise. But none of them seemed to take up their issues with the restaurant first. It was easier to attack the reviewer.

One-off letters, phone calls and emails from angry, possibly deranged diners, proved to be the minority. From book sales close to 40,000 and a readership of the paper of nearly 900,000 a week, any feedback was overwhelmingly positive. People agreed wholeheartedly with the assertion that the service at a slick city lounge bar, Chicane, was pretentious and mean-spirited. The Doyle's review prompted an unprecedented outpouring of responses all thanking me for exploding the myth. Only one email arrived to diss the review. It suggested not that Doyle's, an historic restaurant with a great view where fish and chips costs nearly $30, was better than my review, but argued instead that it was an easy target and that consumer protection was best left to the magazine *Choice*. Dropping Rockpool, a three-hat restaurant, to a vaguely more earthly two hats? Only two voices of complaint, one of which contacted us later and apologised, saying we were right.

The restaurant's responses were, of course, less well tempered, often flecked with barely restrained fury. But it didn't affect the way I would review.

I understand how chefs and restaurateurs work. I've seen the face of unfettered anger in the kitchen. It's usually all forgotten over a couple of shandies at the bar after work. But the true evil ones, the belligerent, coked-up paranoids, don't get over it. They're not just arseholes during service, or when the pressure brings it out. They're not the kind of chef who loses it in the heat of service then buys you a beer ten minutes after you finish work. They're mean-spirited pricks through and through who will shaft not just the reviewer, but also every diner who walks through their front door. The art of hospitality, of course, means that they will smile while they're doing it.

17

The emperor's new restaurant

'YOU'RE SO BRAVE,' people said to me when I reviewed a high-profile chef's restaurant and found it wanting. I hadn't run into a burning house to rescue a child. I was just doing my job.

The declarations of courage came not just from the public and other chefs, but also, amazingly, from the food media. It was as if 'named' chefs should be seen as infallible, and I'd done something they couldn't or wouldn't. Despite doing what I felt any honourable reviewer should do, I was considered plucky. Many people knew the restaurant didn't stack up, but nobody in the food world would say bad things about high-profile chefs. Indeed, some professional food writers would align themselves with celebrity chefs to enhance their own credibility, perpetuating myths instead of applying healthy journalistic scepticism.

No restaurant, and no chef, has a right to expect anything from a reviewer except an honestly held belief, expressed well, and mindful of the facts. If anything, a high-profile chef has more responsibility; the weight of the public's trust is already on their side. They've got to get it right because they, of all people, should know better.

Several high-profile chefs probably thought I derided them in print. As far as I was concerned, nothing was personal, everything based on the way the restaurants ran and the quality of the food they put out. Saying things sucked was what I was paid to do. So long as it did suck. (Although with our defamation laws, saying it sucked probably meant saying it 'could have been better'.) Brittle egos and paranoia, however, meant opinions were often misconstrued as reflections on the chefs as people.

I once had a rather spirited phone call from a well-known chef about a review of his restaurant. He didn't like it. The review, that is. No surprise there, because I didn't like his restaurant much. On this occasion the conversation was remarkably amicable. He and I agreed that some of the food was a bit lacklustre on my visits. We also shared the view that the service had too many hiccups. What we didn't agree on was that I should be able to write about it so vividly. To me, a big-name chef is the same as every-body else, just another dickhett, except the public has higher expectations of them.

I've had way too many arguments with all kinds of restaurant owners over the years. One wanted to impress me with how his chef filleted the fish when other chefs bought theirs in filleted. I just wanted the chef to cook it better. Some felt they should get extra points because they had Limoges porcelain or fancy flatwear (cutlery to you and me), when they couldn't find a waiter who knew their stuff. The worst, of course, were those who had invested substantial amounts of money, usually in second-rate waterside restaurants, and felt that because of their invest-ment I should score them better. In these cases, the water views were like lipstick on a pig, and didn't fool me. The owners of these joints were just cynical business operators, probably better suited to immigration detention centres than the business of putting immaculate fresh ingredients on the plates of discerning diners. Their investment was their responsibility; my responsibility was to my readers.

The responses of well-known chefs, the emperors of Sydney dining, to even a marginally negative review were endlessly fascinating. Happy when I named them for good cooking, they hated being named when the review was unflattering. They were often as insecure about their cooking as the best looking celebrities are about their looks. Only one restaurateur, the late and esteemed Anders Ousback, ever said he thought I'd got it wrong, in that I'd scored his restaurant too high. Others, of course, felt hard done by even when they didn't fail in the score. One restaurant, XO, renamed a dish after me following a review in which I'd called it greasy and silly. No matter that for the previous eight years I'd written about several dozen of Neil Perry's other dishes and raved – the stupid one I despised was graced with my name.

Another high-profile restaurant I reviewed wrote and accused me of being 'unAustralian', whatever that's supposed to mean, shooting the messenger rather than dealing with the smell of ammonia in their fish.

One well-known, longstanding restaurant family reduced my editor to tears. She took up their offer to meet as a conciliatory gesture and to explain why the newspaper had run such a harsh review. Rubbishy food was a good start. Oh, and two-tiered service depending on who you were. More than one staffer on the newspaper had visited this restaurant to confirm the review. I spoke to the editor as she left the meeting, rattled and shocked by treatment that would surprise no-one who has worked in hospitality. The fact they went in for intimidation says a lot about them and their attitude. They're still taking customers today.

One highly anticipated restaurant decided to 'motivate' its staff by slagging me off. I understood that my name was mud to many chefs, but I didn't expect them to make up stuff to try and win over the people who worked for them. I started to get phone calls and emails from customers who had been told that I had a vendetta against the chef. Waiters wanted to write 'Heckler' columns for the newspaper about personal bias.

Interestingly enough, restaurant complainants never addressed my ability to write, or the score alone, merely offering cheap and unsubstantiated jibes at my credibility. I'm as open as you can be to criticism of my craft, but attack my integrity and you'll have a fight on your hands.

It wasn't just restaurants that tried cheap jibes. A competing newspaper ran a campaign to discredit me after I'd written about Doyle's. They abandoned it when they found more people in favour of my review than against. I later chanced on the journalist they'd sent to give it a write-up, who agreed with my verdict and decided not to go into print.

Admittedly, most responses from restaurants, when they responded, were quite fair. Some rang to ask how they could improve. One high-profile chef wrote a note of such unbearable sadness that I felt guilty, until I remembered the lacklustre food he'd been offering of late. Another restaurateur at Berowra Waters Inn nearly went broke, and later wrote to offer his thanks after a more positive review two years later. 'It would have been cheaper,' he said, 'to just buy you a house' – and get an honest opinion, privately, in the first place.

I welcomed feedback, especially when it was soundly argued. I wanted to hear from people when they'd had markedly different experiences to my own, or when I made mistakes identifying ingredients. It was always good to get a response from a restaurant after a review, good or bad. I liked receiving correspondence from the staff of restaurants. A waitress named Yolanda wrote to apologise for the sullen service in a restaurant where I'd found some waiters wanting. It was touching, especially considering she was outstanding and it was the male waiters who needed a rocket up the date, or at least a smile transplant. Other waiters were sacked after negative reviews – in my opinion the wrong way to fix a problem. Management, be it in the kitchen or on the floor, are always responsible for standards. They do the hiring, the training, and the staffing. More than once I was brought into the fringes of unfair dismissal cases by sacked staff.

While angry chefs are one thing, unhinged restaurateurs are the critic's main worry. Some bragged about having my private address and phone number. One abusive caller rang while I was out of the country on a break. He couldn't accept that I wasn't avoiding his calls, I was just out of town. 'I'll give you one more chance to get it right,' he warned me about my review. Thing is, I didn't need another chance. You should've seen the review before the lawyers took the sting out.

Interestingly for me, the critical barbs about reviews and reviewing sometimes came from the food media. Disgruntled, jaded ex-reviewers were the most surprising. One wrote in print about the demotion of Neil Perry's Rockpool from three hats to two: 'He deserves better than the shabby treatment dished up to him.' Curiously this same critic was adamant that free speech should be protected during his tenure, when he was as likely to comment on the waiters' polyester shirts as anything culinary. He's the same critic who admitted, in print, that he doesn't find broad beans have much taste. Another, who edits a restaurant guide where they don't necessarily visit the restaurants every year, called for my resignation after I appeared on *Heat in the Kitchen*.

My immediate predecessor, Terry Durack, however, distinguished himself by his silence. A man whose advice came rarely and in small doses was eloquent in his absence, in his ability to let a new voice come to the task of reviewing. To this day I thank him for it. Fortunately, there was also a handful of upper echelon Sydney reviewers who seemed happy to disagree at times, while retaining dignity and professionalism.

When I took the job as reviewer I said I was in awe of our chefs, but wouldn't be overawed by them. Thankfully, I never lost my love of great food, or of marvellous restaurants. There were always great, positive places to eat where talent didn't hinge on an unstable ego.

These restaurants were the ones that rocked my world. I was overjoyed talking to French expats about the deftness and subtlety of the food at Marque, a restaurant that attained three-hat status during my editorship. I rejoiced in the incredible fire and brimstone at Thai exponents Spice I Am. There was much shock and awe thanks to Peter Gilmore's genius with textures at Quay. At the same time there was the incomparable cooking of seafood at a modest fish caff, Fish Face, and the comforting richness of regional stayer The Old George and Dragon.

I found inordinate amounts of delight in both exposing overrated restaurants and supporting underrated ones. Australian food has come such a long way. The food I once learnt to cook would turn stomachs in many Australian restaurants today, in part because diners demand food that's so much better. And celebrity chefs have had a part in that. Every time a Jamie, Bill or Gordon cooks in front of an audience, something sinks in, which means better food at home and higher expectations when we eat out. What it doesn't mean is that the food at a famous chef's restaurant will always be exemplary. Or that the truth about that will always win out.

18

Stoned to death for defamation

YOU'D THINK WRITING a restaurant review was pretty straightforward. Well, nobody told the courts, and the way defamation law works in this country means that no review is ever completely honest.

As innocuous as they may seem, restaurant reviews are a magnet for litigation. Leo the Lobster, as one case is colloquially known, resulted after a predecessor at the *Herald*, Leo Schofield, referred to lobsters at the Blue Angel as 'broiled'. A hundred thousand dollars was awarded against *The Sydney Morning Herald* in 1989. Another reviewer didn't like the cutlery he thought let down a North Shore eatery. John Newton's March 1993 review cost Fairfax, the *Herald*'s owner, another cool $180,000 – plus costs – when it reached court in February 1997. Those two cases, and others that never went to court, make publishing houses extremely nervous about restaurant reviews. If you think chefs are on edge before a review comes out, you should see how jumpy the lawyers get.

My court case, the one that still lingers like the smell of Limburger as I write, has already cost more in legal fees than I ever earnt writing reviews for the newspaper. And the case against me is still running.

Defamation is a curious beast. Until early 2006 'truth' wasn't even a defence. No matter that the waiter was rude, the pasta soggy, the steak acrid; in a court of law truth didn't stand up. Saying someone had been to prison, when they had been to prison, used to be enough to get you a lawsuit. Sure, there are other defences, such as public interest and opinion, but criticising someone's business is fraught with legal issues. The legal system works against honest, open, fair-minded restaurant reviews that call it like it is.

When I started reviewing full-time my boss at the time didn't think I should be too concerned. 'Say what you think,' he encouraged, 'and our lawyers will change anything that will get us in trouble. We take on the Prime Minister and BHP, we aren't going to be scared by a restaurant.'

It was a good way to approach it: write what you believed should be said, don't pull punches, then find out what is legally acceptable when you see the final copy. Reassuringly, the newspaper would pay for any legal action. Over time I worked out ways to say things that the lawyers didn't find as much fault with, but there was hardly a week where they didn't have some changes, perhaps just a rewording of a sentence or two.

Criticisms were always tempered. Instead of saying the pasta was overcooked I'd have to say the pasta was, in my opinion, cooked for perhaps a little longer than it needed to be so it was soggy and falling apart. Instead of saying the waiter was an arrogant prick who looked at me like I was shit on a shoe, I'd have to suggest that maybe they'd had a bad day. Or maybe it was something I'd said. Instead of the salad tasting like compost, the soup being reminiscent of a stagnant pond, or the fish smelling like a sewerage outfall, I'd have to say they weren't to my taste; they were disappointing. Or perhaps they let down the meal, or could have been better. Instead of saying that a chef who uses truffle oil and charges $50 for the dish is a rip-off merchant, I'd have to say $50 seems excessive, or ambitious, or the prices seem designed with the bank manager, rather than the customer, in mind. Even then I was unlikely to get most of what I really thought in print.

Part of it is a cultural thing; each editor has their own slant on what's in good taste or humour. Don't slag off Parramatta, I was told, despite it being shamefully bad as a place to dine considering its huge population and income. Don't have a go at stuck-up eastern suburbs eateries, or surfie hangouts where all they want is wedges and caesar salad. And don't say you don't care about the chef — he's famous, you know.

But much of the editing is also for legal reasons. Every single word of every single review I wrote was run past the legal team. The review's weekly summary, the four hundred or so reviews in *The Good Food Guide*, the restaurant that scored 19 out of 20 and the one that scored 7 out of 20; all of them were run past expert defamation lawyers, and this book has been too. Why? Because restaurants sue, and the law lets them.

I first ate at Coco Roco, on the western cusp of the CBD, in the spring of 2003. A swank new place with water views, the menu sounded okay, if not inspiring, when the PR firm sent it to me for a read. The location had a lot to recommend it, too, tucked in the newly bustling, previously untapped waterside location of King Street Wharf. It was a posh place where the Serbian expat owners had spent three million dollars on the fitout.

But after two meals, both of which left me as cold as a snot-nose trevalla, I filed a review that pointed out their decent cooking of steak, but some pretty serious failings in other areas.

In my 800 or so words, I didn't criticise everything I found distasteful. I didn't like all the food. I liked the view, but found some service a bit dozy. And I wrote about it. The lawyers shredded my original piece, cutting parts until they were happy. I was used to the changes, and you don't argue when you're being protected from court action.

Yet despite our best efforts, the restaurant still sued. I wound up with a private investigator, reportedly, looking into my past, a series of farcical accusations by the plaintiffs and a barrister who opened his case by suggesting that 'defendants are stoned to death for defamation in Serbia and Montenegro.'

When the news broke that the owners of Coco Roco were considering legal action, it wasn't a comfortable time. National current affairs television shows wanted to run with the story, *The Bulletin* approached me with a series of accusations which appeared to have been lifted from Coco Roco's ludicrous series of claims. Radio stations wanted to air stories on the case. Maybe the restaurant's owners couldn't see it, but the court case cemented the name of Coco Roco in everybody's heads as a place that copped a bad review. Other eateries came and went, or came and stayed, but the court case has ensured that Coco Roco will always be thought of as a dodgy restaurant. I bet no-one can remember the name of the other restaurant I scored 9 out of 20.

Some of what the restaurateurs alleged would have made good reading – if I wasn't so worried about the attacks on my credibility, the hours I'd have to spend preparing for possible legal action, or the associated publicity and smear campaign. Someone with a hankering for a more public profile might even have enjoyed the notoriety. For me it has been at times quite a burden to bear.

Eventually Coco Roco closed. All up it had been running ten months, nearly two months before and eight months after my review was published. They filed for defamation before the courts.

When the threat of a lawsuit and accusations of malice first hit the news, *The Sydney Morning Herald* went very quiet on the matter. I was left with a sinking feeling in my stomach. My name was being besmirched in print by other publications and the people who employed me had nothing to say. There was an undercurrent of suspicion and for a while I didn't feel safe. Not professionally, and not personally. Blame it on the man who spent the better part of three months loitering at the entrance to my street. Blame it on the quarter-page picture of me in *The Daily Telegraph*, or their series of stories alleging, among other things, that I'd visited on the second night after the place opened. After Coco Roco closed, the restaurant's own PR company made legal moves to claim back unpaid moneys, but not before they'd had a swipe at my credibility.

Thanks to the publicity, people started to recognise me in the street and wanted to talk about the case. Restaurateurs thought it funny to bring the topic up. I overheard conversations about it in restaurants and cafés. My friends rallied around, but I felt professionally isolated.

I was used to being talked about rather than talked to, but this took the whole nature of reviewing and amplified it tenfold. I felt under fire. All the while the *Herald* kept its own counsel.

It turns out that my own newspaper was also investigating me. I guess they couldn't know my background, or my values, until they'd checked me out. It still stung. Once they'd done their homework, however, they came out to defend me, and my review. Sadly, even after being investigated, I couldn't talk about the details to other publications, to the television and radio stations, but I could say we believed in the accuracy of the review. The occasional snipe continued to appear in other media, but at least I knew I had support.

One good thing did come out of the hoo-ha. I took a long, hard look at myself. The sad thing, really, is a feeling that any private investigators would have little to find. Nothing unusual or sordid in my background, no bribery or blackmail, no secret friendships with chefs, or raging vendettas; a pretty boring existence, really, and one that I made a mental note to try and change. As Socrates said, an unexamined life is not worth living. But I'm not sure, even now, that mine is worth examining.

In their statement of claim, Coco Roco suggested that a reference to black reflector tiles in the bathrooms meant that I thought they were suitable for homosexuals. They asserted that they weren't 'black reflector tiles' anyway, but rather black tiles 'with a high gloss finish'. They also claimed 'apricots in sherry-scented white sauce with prime-ribbed steak is a well-known dish available in leading restaurants in Europe.' Each to their own, I guess.

The whole thing seems farcical if you're not involved and one day I hope to laugh freely about it. It's just that that particular day is yet to arrive.

Since the case is still before the courts, parts of this story must remain untold. I can say that my review called Coco Roco a 'bleak spot on the culinary landscape', and I stand by that.

On 1 June 2005, unusually for me, I was wearing a suit. In court. Not just any suit, but an expensive number that the newspaper bought for the launch of the twentieth anniversary *Good Food Guide* in September 2004. Sick of my own attempts to dress, management decided I'd be better togged up by someone with more taste in clothes, and a bigger budget. Given a few more court appearances, one day the suit will actually pay its way.

Even my lawyer didn't recognise me when I showed up in something other than a T-shirt. Maybe I hadn't needed a disguise at restaurants after all, just a better tailor. There was no urgent need for me to be in court; at a first hearing before a jury, only the words of the review are considered, not evidence. But the lawyers wanted me there, and I wanted to see how it all worked.

The NSW Supreme Court building is a massive, relatively windowless (and aesthetically void) monolith on Macquarie Street in Sydney. Security was tight; we handed in our small arms at the metal detectors on the ground floor and ended up several floors above in one of the modest rooms where civil justice is done in this state.

Three people, Aleksandra and Ljiljana Gacic and Branislav Ciric, were suing Fairfax Publications and myself for the review published on 30 September 2003. The case appeared before a four-person jury nearly two years after the review was published. In NSW this trial decides if a matter is defamatory. If it is, there's another trial to decide if there should be damages. At the second trial we could argue things like fair comment and opinion, and they would try to show inaccuracies, damage to their business and malice. It's at a second trial that I would give evidence.

I sat near the defence team – on the opposite side to the three restaurateurs, presumably. Three people on the other side did glare at my friends and I, avoiding us in the lobby and at doorways. We hovered tentatively at the elevators come recess; there's etiquette to court hearings, and sharing a lift with your adversaries on the way to the top-floor café just doesn't cut it.

Justice Virginia Bell had a sprightly look and sparkling eyes. She resembled a bird as she peered out from underneath her fine-curled judicial wig, the classic garb symbolising the removal of personal prejudice and the wearing of the authority of the law. I reckon it made her look older than she probably was, adding a maturity and gravitas dyed hair probably wouldn't achieve. I imagined her ripping the wig off to reveal bright blue locks and tearing off her robe to expose a hot red skirt suit. But that's just me. It was Justice Bell's job to deal with the law, the jury's to deal with the facts.

It was a tense room, but remarkably low key, the legal team softly spoken, the seats around us virtually all empty. For a case I'd been dreading for the better part of two years, one everybody wanted to put on telly or in print when it first made the news, it was an anticlimax.

Four men filed in from the right-hand side to the jury box; one in a footy jersey, another a tracksuit top. They looked like I might, if I wasn't in court (and if I didn't have a suit bought for me). They represented the Ordinary Reasonable Reader, the mythical fair-minded person who reads the newspaper on a regular or irregular basis, who has all sorts of information sources and a critical brain. It was these four men who would decide whether the review was defamatory.

They heard from an ancient, authoritative-looking barrister for the plaintiffs, Clive Evatt, who leant on the podium, wheezed a little and appealed to their sense of the common man. His approach was a shock. Instead of trying to convince the jury that the restaurant was good, he suggested it was bad. Inordinately bad. 'It's bad eating,' he said. 'It's horrifyingly bad. Distasteful, disagreeable, unpalatable.'

The trick must have been to disgust the jury. While the former restaurateurs looked on, he drove home the grimness of the review by saying how bad the restaurant sounds. 'If Coco Roco scored nine out of twenty,' Evatt reasoned, 'and twenty out twenty is "Heaven", we're a bit closer to hell.'

How I wish I'd been able to say that in print.

The jury heard line after line of the review being read out, accompanied by some argument to convince them it was defamatory. It sounded horrible broken down like that. I wanted to edit the review, rewrite it, to make it more concise and pointed as they spoke. Nearly two years after being written and legalled, it sounded dull, equivocal, guarded.

Tom Blackburn was the fresh-faced barrister representing Fairfax and myself. He seemed remarkably upbeat and

227

yet calm, almost quiet before the bench. He often rocked up onto his toes, hands in pockets, looking like a cheeky boy. He pointed out to the jury that it's just a restaurant review; it's just one person's opinion.

The jury were instructed in matters of law, defamation was defined for them again, and they were sent to consider a verdict. They didn't take long. Yes, the review did say that Coco Roco served unpalatable food. Yes, Coco Roco offered some bad service, but neither claim was defamatory. And on the other two counts, that Coco Roco charged excessive prices and that the owners were incompetent as restaurateurs – it was a resounding 'no'. We had won.

You'd hope a restaurant that scores 9 out of 20 and a 'stay home' recommendation had scored so low for reasons to do with the food and service rather than the colour of the paint work. But it was wonderful to think you could be critical without it being defamatory.

On hearing the verdict, the weight fell from my shoulders like leaden pastry from pie. One restaurateur gasped and clutched a manicured hand to her mouth as she ran from the court. I certainly didn't feel victorious, just overcome with relief. From my point of view there was nothing to win, really, just a lot to lose by being thrust into the public eye yet again. Oh, and being continuously hamstrung when writing reviews.

As we debriefed outside the court, a swarthy man loitered, strangely alone and aimless, just within earshot. He then followed us downstairs and lingered nearby as three of us parted company. If he was interested in me, he followed the wrong person home.

✻

A few months later, I called Mark Polden, my defamation lawyer at Fairfax, for an opinion on another review. 'Coco Roco is appealing' he said, and he didn't mean attractive.

Unfortunately, winning that first jury trial wasn't the end of it. On 31 March 2006 we were back in the Supreme Court building, in a smaller, more airless courtroom with purple chairs and dark wood panelling. Behind the bench was the coat of arms, bearing a lion and a unicorn. Court assistants awaited and we all rose when the judges entered the room.

The three judges of the Appeal Court seemed vastly different from each other. Justice Beazley asked pointed, vigorous questions. Justice Ipp on the right-hand side looked tired. He buried his head in his hands, staring at the pages on the desk in front of him. Often he took his substantial hand and rubbed up underneath his glasses. He was probably deep in thought, but to an outsider it looked as if he was bored or hung over; the top of his pale wig was often more visible than his face. Justice Handley, like the other two, often sat with one finger to his cheek and a fist in front of his mouth as he listened to arguments from counsel.

Two of the plaintiffs, the women, watched pensively from across the room. It must have been incredibly tough for them. They sat, legs pressed tightly together, lips pursed. One had her hands folded guardedly over a bag in her lap, hair firmly pulled back, a picture of tense elegance.

The restaurateurs' barrister Clive Evatt argued that the jury's verdict, stating that the restaurant had served some unpalatable food and offered some bad service, automatically meant his clients had been defamed. He performed like a doddery old man, as if he, one of defamation's sharpest minds, had been outsmarted.

Justice Ipp seemed to have already made up his mind. 'It's very hard to believe that wouldn't be defamatory,' he said at one point, after a line was read from my review.

Our legal team spent most of the day writing like demons, constantly grabbing old and important-looking law texts from the trolley while Evatt spoke. I sat, nervous, intrigued, out of my depth and awestruck. I watched as the miracle of western justice moved in achingly slow, seemingly pointless fashion, arguing about the minutest of details. It seemed like such a waste of time and money, but the option, I thought as I watched Iraq burn each night on the television, is not an option.

When Tom Blackburn stood to argue our side of the case, the judges seemed immediately antagonistic. To some in the legal profession, criticism, by its very nature, is defamatory.

Then a turnaround, it seemed. 'If this is defamatory,' Ipp said at one point, 'it must make writing a restaurant review impossible.'

By the second day of the appeal, Blackburn's trolley of books contained a further seventeen legal texts, littered with over sixty orange Post-it notes highlighting relevant legal precedents. He referred back to a decision made in 1928, then to one from the late 1700s. He went back through our legal history to prove a point. Justice Ipp seemed annoyed by the complexity of the law, referring to it as a 'mystical, esoteric regime known only to the high priests'.

One hour and forty minutes after the first argument had been put on the second day of the trial, the court adjourned. The three judges reserved their decision. It was going to be two months, at least, before we knew our fate.

'Have you ever had a special leave before?' asked Mark Polden on the telephone.

'To be honest,' I replied, 'I don't make a habit of being sued.'

Almost to the day, three months after Coco Roco's appeal, the three judges handed down their thirty-five page decision. They'd sent one part of the case back for a retrial, and overturned the jury's decision on the other two — that Coco Roco served unpalatable food and had some bad service — finding them defamatory. That meant we had lost the preliminary case and would have to offer a full defence.

Our legal advice, however, suggested that the appeal court erred. They had taken too much power into their hands. They should only overturn a decision, we reasoned, if no jury in their right mind should have found the imputations non-defamatory. They didn't have to like the jury's decision (and they didn't: as they put it, 'no jury, properly directed, could reasonably reach any other verdict'), but as judges deal with law, not fact, we thought they should wear it. The interpretation came down to was the jury 'properly directed' and there was thousands of dollars of legal argument in that alone.

In July 2006 we filed a special leave application before the High Court of Australia, the big court on the shore of Lake Burley Griffin in Canberra; the one you may remember from the movie *The Castle*. It's the court that only hears interesting cases, those that have large ramifications for other parts of the law. The High Court makes judgements that set very strong precedents, acting as a kind of overseer of the state courts.

In June 2007 the High Court decision from a February hearing of the full bench went six judges to one against us. Apart from the dissenting judge, Michael Kirby, the others reinforced the appeal court's view, that any criticism is defamatory. It makes a critic's job hard, really. The case was aired in the US, the UK, China and on blogs around the world. *The Australian* newspaper ran an editorial covering it, as did the *Herald*, even though it was just a court upholding the status quo. The favoured quote in most stories was Kirby's: 'On subjects such as a criticism of a restaurant's food and service, lay jurors are much more likely to reflect community standards than judges.'

His solo voice, of course, was swamped by six others. The end result of our High Court appeal is that there will be a further jury trial to decide, once again, whether my review accused the restaurateurs of being incompetent. Once that is over, I will be up in court in yet another trial, this time before a judge, to give evidence at last. It will take at least until mid 2008 before the whole thing has been dealt with — nearly five years after the review first appeared. Appealing the appeal has ended up prolonging the agony. With each month the relevance of the review to my current life becomes more tenuous.

I'm happy to stand up in court and justify myself, even if it does involve that Hugo Boss suit yet again. From what I can gather, it will make for interesting reading. I'm more than comfortable with the Coco Roco review that appeared in print. I just wish the courts would hurry up

and get on with it. If we succeed in defending the defamation action, it could redefine the rules for restaurant critics
– and what diners are allowed to read – in this country.
You never know, it might even mean that reviewers no
longer fear being stoned to death, too.

19

Why I like to eat at home now

AFTER FIVE YEARS, nearly 2500 meals and about 750 long and short reviews as *The Sydney Morning Herald*'s Chief Restaurant Reviewer, in late 2005 I resigned. It was time to go. I felt on top of the game, able to write confidently about Sydney restaurants and their place in the city and the world. I'd given the highest and lowest scores of my career in the space of one year. I held no fear of chefs, or their lawyers. Assertions that I'd scored too highly or had been too churlish were roughly equal in number, so it seemed I'd stumbled upon some modicum of balance. We'd won the defamation case (though I knew Coco Roco was appealing), and it was important to leave with some public trust still on my side. My last few months of reviews were also distinguished by the most consistently good restaurants I'd encountered in five years. It just felt right.

I gave three months' notice, my departure cloaked in secrecy. The last thing I wanted was for restaurants to know I was going. In one last act of bastardry to those who were still busy sucking up or wasting energy hating me, my resignation was kept under wraps until after my successor, Simon Thomsen, had already started to eat out.

In my final week in the job, the *Herald* kindly gave me the cover story of the 'Good Living' liftout, allowing me to distil some of what I'd learnt about restaurants in my time. The cover sported a picture of me shot from behind, wine glass in hand, and with six chef's knives thrust in my back.

It was apt in more ways than one. Quitting reviewing did feel like having a knife thrust between my shoulder blades, even if it was me who put it there. It was like the loss of a lover. Restaurants are hard to give up. They had shaped me (back pain and all) for most of my adult life. I'd moved from working in kitchens to working in dining rooms with hardly a pause. Suddenly my thirty hours a week spent in restaurants (plus travelling, thinking and writing time) was slashed to virtually none. I stepped from an exhausting but reasonable paying job into relative poverty and obscurity. Keeping my resignation a secret meant I couldn't look for work, and wasn't swamped with offers. I went from being a widely read commentator to a man scratching around for a column.

When I took on the chief reviewer's job, I promised I wouldn't outstay my welcome. Having observed not just restaurants but also their critics, I realised that most reviewers start to believe their own bullshit after a few years. I'd watched my predecessors and brethren in the trade and thought that some stayed too long. Five to seven years seemed an appropriate length of time in the job; any longer and it's unlikely a reviewer is in it for the passion, or putting in enough hours and miles to justify the alleged power that goes with territory. Certainly in Sydney with its high profile and high demands.

When I started writing there weren't many people who made a proper living freelance writing about food, and virtually no full-time restaurant reviewers. I took a punt, spending all I'd earned and putting a somewhat promising professional life as a chef on the line. It paid off. I got the best job I could ask for. By age forty I may not have achieved all I dreamt I could do, like joining the KISS Army, winning an Olympic medal, or shagging Naomi Watts, but I had managed to do the kind of work I had long lusted after.

Restaurant reviewers are restaurant sluts. For years I'd chased the youngest, the most enticing, the shiniest. I was promiscuous, always on the lookout for the next, the newest, the brightest. Some people thought giving it up was the culinary equivalent of breaking up with Megan Gale. But if restaurants were my mistress, they wanted too much in return for their favours. Yes, they did make me deliriously, deliciously happy. They satisfied a certain neediness by taking me out in the evenings, blowing my mind in all kinds of ways. The sights, sounds and smells were utterly intoxicating and the mood invigorating. Hospitality still, when it's good, sends a little quiver down my spine.

Leaving that behind was hard, but it was also the best thing to do. Now I can settle down with restaurants I actually like. I can hate a restaurant for no reason at all, or love one without having to justify it. I can eat at home, and enjoy a purity of flavour that even the best restaurants can't manage. Now that I no longer have the most expensive shit in Sydney, I've rediscovered evenings of leisure, and mornings where I wake up famished. I've discovered that weekends aren't just a time to head north, or south or west to find yet another new restaurant, but a time to catch up with mates, or simply (and this is the best bit) plan nothing.

Without the annual pressures of *The Good Food Guide*, I've filled my life with normal things – reading, telly, walking, socialising, bands, movies, and travel to places I like rather than to restaurants I hope I'll like. I now greet the day with a clearer head, the stultifying effects of wine and rich food no longer a problem. I sleep better because I seldom have a 'food hangover'. My skin is clearer, my eyes brighter, my outlook more positive than it has been for years. I no longer answer the phone expecting an aggressive restaurateur on the other end. The kilos have fallen from me like truffle oil from a chef's tablespoon. I now look gangly again, and my clothes are baggy, but I feel terrific. I'm down from ninety-eight kilos to about eighty-two, from size thirty-eight to a size thirty-two (on a good day). It's true, restaurants do make you fat.

I now enjoy an aching, bone-deep hunger that for so long was absent. I love saying no to dessert. Or only having dessert. I delight in eating risotto that isn't finished with too much cream or butter because the chef was too lazy to stir it to order from the beginning. I'm rediscovering vegetables – and not woody carrots, old bok choi or starchy beans that cost $8 a bowl. Sandwiches have reappeared on my radar, and Vegemite toast is a regular fixture in the weekly diet.

For someone who just loved dining out, it's hard to believe how much I enjoy dining in. More than ever I'm a fan of the flavour of home-cooked food, and I'm constantly amazed that restaurants can't achieve it. Living close to a decent greengrocer, foraging in the suburbs for olives and lemons and mandarins, and having a plot in a community garden, I often have access to produce as good as the best restaurants. Restaurant food is usually prepared ahead then kept for hours – if not days – before it's cooked or reheated. Home cooking, my home cooking and my friends', tastes more like the real ingredients, more true to the produce. It's like eating with the volume turned up.

Life these days is much simpler and more meaningful. The people who ring me up are true friends not just people sucking up. I have more time to forge relationships, to cure my own olives, make my own tomato passata, to test self-saucing chocolate pudding recipes just because I want to eat the end result.

I still adore restaurants. Good ones. And I have a particular soft spot for places where it's possible to sit in million-dollar locations, use cutlery and glassware you can't afford and partake of world-class food and wine delivered by witty, intelligent waiters. I still think this is one of the most stimulating experiences a dag from Canberra can enjoy. I'm just not in lust with restaurants any more. I want less frantic clothes-tearing and more credibility, more stability, more resonance with real life.

I don't miss bad restaurants at all. I don't miss the endless procession of dreary restaurants not bad enough to slag off and not good enough to rave about. I don't miss formulaic restaurants or the disingenuous service offered at some places once I was recognised. I don't miss the drudge of putting together *The Good Food Guide*, or the mindless invective that came my way. And I certainly don't miss the constant question: 'Where can I take my girlfriend for dinner?' It's an impossible thing to answer unless I know your budget, your tastes, your usual dining habits, your location and your short list. Surely you've made one.

There's this restaurant guide I know that includes hundreds of recommendations every year.

The new life, as I expected, is much quieter. I've stepped from a cyclone of meals, lawyers, editors and hundreds of articles a year into the calm of middle age, where the mobile hardly rings, editors rarely return my calls, and my bank balance is suffering. My inbox, once full of recommendations and insults, is strangely empty.

On the upside, I've acquired the best lifestyle. I can visit my parents on the south coast midweek. I can drop in on a leatherwood honey producer in Tassie or go and hand-milk cows in Western Australia. Each morning on my walk near the water I plan what to have for dinner and shop at the specialists that line my local high street. I have more time to make my own pizza dough, to cook for those I adore and to savour the sociability of food, arguably its greatest attraction. What's more, I have another great love in my life, a relationship I'm trying really hard not to stuff up.

Surprisingly, there's a lot of goodwill still coming my way from people who once read my reviews, amazingly not all of it from the punters. I've even been given the opportunity to do a variety of work, some at the very restaurants I'd been reviewing. It's hard to believe I ever found the time to do what I did.

Having often felt like an auditor, I never expected a chef's welcome to be any warmer than the one they'd give to the health inspector. So it's been a delight to find that many former adversaries are not adversaries at all. Since I was able to drop my blanket rule about not fraternising with chefs, several have invited me to come for a meal as their guest to show off what they're cooking these days. That's pure hospitality at work: simple honour and generosity. Others have made a point of just shaking my hand. It's been a pleasure to come out the other side and realise that most decent restaurants are run by decent people. Some crap restaurants are run by decent people, too.

On the eve of the 2007 *Good Food Guide* awards, I received a message on my mobile phone. 'I hope you've got a bullet-proof vest,' it said, in an Italian accent as thick and rich as tiramisu.

For a moment my heart stopped. It was nine months since I'd left the job and the 2007 *Guide* wasn't my baby, but I'd recently been privy to some creepy evidence of a smear campaign and threats from a restaurateur with a longstanding grudge.

The call turned out to be a dinner invitation. From a chef, as it happens. Not a wild, paranoid, knife-wielding, gun-toting, drug-addled troll. Just someone with a sense of humour. Someone who knew well the dark, depraved, exhilarating, euphoric, bitter, brilliant, disappointing, nervy, miraculous terrain of restaurant land – and all who inhabit it.

For me, the most interesting realisation after relinquishing the job was that I have more in common with chefs than I do most other people. For all the craziness, the paranoia and the ego, some just cook because they love it. We're bound by this love of flavour, a passion for great food and wondrous restaurants, and an obsessive search for perfection, be it in something as humble as an artichoke or as esteemed as a truffle.

Like all passionate people, we can be misunderstood. I don't mind being known as a food snob, or even a food wanker, but it's a shame that caring about how food is reared, treated, cooked and served is considered unusual in this country. I'm pretty sure if I was as passionate about footy as I am about food, I'd be celebrated. If it was computers, I'd be loaded. If it was trains, I'd be lonely.

Despite the great advances in the food scene over the last twenty years, Australia still has a way to go. There are plenty of voyeuristic foodies who pore daily over glossy food mags, but many of them don't aspire (or expect) to eat well at every meal. Most Australians eat far too much sugar and processed food, at home and out. We're morbidly obese as a nation. What's more, there isn't a culturally embedded reverence and respect for ingredients as there is in true food nations like Japan, China, Thailand, Italy and France.

We are, however, blessed to have the influences of those nations and their culinary genius, be it as sang choi bau or pasta. Hot and sour prawn soup sits perfectly with an Australian rainforest view, as does Sardinian-style fried calamari overlooking a beach. The impact of multicultur-alism on our tastebuds is unquestionable and we can cherry-pick the best.

But I worry about where our food is heading, as restaur-ants try too hard to cook strange food: food that's foamed and tampered with and mucked about. I've always thought most chefs are far better off surfing for a couple of hours than fiddling with the ingredients. A few masters have proved me wrong, but even in our top tier we're now seeing food that isn't as yummy, as plainly good as it should be. There's too much fussy stuff deconstructed on square plates rather than just great-tasting tucker. While there are more top-end restaurants than there were five years ago, with high-end prices to match, the focus on making food complicated rather than scrumptious has led to a drop in standards at the cutting edge. Icarus-style chefs are stretching beyond their capabilities, and beyond the talent of their team.

And nobody's saying a thing.

At the risk of never working again, I'll let you in on a secret. The food media in general are frightened of those who cook for a living. Chefs can be menacing people, thanks to the bullyboy tactics learnt in the heat of the kitchen. Some of the food media sleep with them, literally. Some suck up to them. Some comply just to avoid having hassles in their lives, or because they need chefs' quotes every time they sell a story. Proper, informed criticism rather than petty, ignorant carping is a rare thing. No wonder chefs aren't used to it.

The dearth of well-articulated, fearless reviews and reviewers prepared to make enemies is a sign of our immaturity as a foodie nation. Most magazines and newspapers run fluff pieces – articles that promote the chefs and their restaurants rather than well-considered journalism with a healthy dose of scepticism. Cooks are surprised when they can't use reviews as publicity tools. Some chefs probably believe their own PR, but that doesn't mean the rest of us have to.

For years I've pushed for better tucker as both chef and writer and I'll continue to do so. I believe that food has a resonance in the whole of our lives. Eating – the aroma, the feel, the placing of food in your mouth – is one of the most sensual things you can do. It's certainly the most personal thing I want to write about. I'm now focused on writing books and articles designed to keep all the bastards involved in food production honest, rather than wishy-washy commentary that perpetuates the status quo. I hope I'll find editors brave enough to publish them. I never really liked trains.

Epilogue
Things they don't tell you when you book

FROM MY DECADE of professional eating out, and my time as a cook, I've learnt a few things about dining. Here are a few tips on how to get the best, avoid the worst, and make the most of a restaurant.

The number of things on the menu is inversely proportional to the WOW factor
The more dishes a menu holds, the thinner any chef's talent has been spread. This doesn't always hold true of Chinese restaurants, but it's certainly true of western restaurants.

Be rude in a Chinese restaurant
That way they'll know you're serious. Waiters are considered quite low in the Chinese hierarchy and an adversarial approach is expected to get results. Refuse the first table you're offered in favour of a better one, even if it's not better. This shows you're in charge. Always order a live fish steamed with ginger and shallots and always choose a Chinese restaurant that is full of Chinese-speaking people. They're nothing

if not devoted to their cuisine. The Chinese even have a word for the kind of restaurants they love, *renau*, meaning 'hot and noisy' – which is a compliment.

Avoid Italian restaurants that put chicken in their pasta
There are a few classic Italian pasta dishes that use chicken, but most Aussie-Italo restaurants that have penne with pollo are bodgy Italians. Also avoid any that use much cream in the pasta or serve anything alfredo. Don't just avoid restaurants that offer a choice of pasta shapes with a choice of sauce, actively try to put them out of business. What's more, don't expect too much of Aussie Italian places. Ours are rarely full of recent immigrants because they can eat far better Italian at home. Even better still is dinner at nonna's home. If you know an Italian, angle for an invite.

Never go out to eat on Valentine's Day
In the industry it's known as Amateur Night: the day when all the people feeling guilty or inadequate or just sucked in by the media campaign decide to visit a restaurant.

Most decent restaurants hate the night and charge accordingly. A space that could seat 100 now only seats fifty or sixty at tables of two. The normally food-hungry crowd is now half made up of women who don't want to eat much. They're watching their figures, you see. Anyone who's being paid for may be a little shy of ordering a decent drink. And the profit margin will fall. Restaurants will want to charge you a set price, give you a glass of champagne (actually a rough drop from Australia) and restrict your menu choices.

Many of the couples are in awkward show-off mode

and think being rude to a waiter is the way to do it. Some are just in the wrong restaurant, a result of consumer-driven insecurity over the whole Valentine thingy. They'll have booked a restaurant posher than they're comfortable in and probably won't be enjoying themselves, which just unnerves everybody, staff and other customers alike.

If you really want to show someone you care, you'll stay in. If you are invited to someone's house, eat heartily. It's a good sign.

Conversation is never private in a restaurant

Every time you say something in a restaurant, a waiter probably overhears. If they don't, the other customers do. So if you want to conduct a private meeting, or say things to a lover you'd rather weren't sniggered over behind the swing doors to the kitchen, then get a private room or eat at home.

Don't order chicken on a Monday

The best, smaller chicken companies usually don't supply the wholesalers on a Monday. That means the chicken in the restaurant fridge (usually sweating in a plastic bag) on a Monday is the one that may have been ordered the previous Friday. Or perhaps Thursday. Or Wednesday.

For instance, in Sydney you can only get Glenloth's excellent free-range chicken FRESH on a Wednesday, according to my wholesaler. I only buy Oak's organic chickens from Tuesday each week as they don't arrive at the butcher's until then. Thirlmere, another top brand, are available from the wholesalers on a Tuesday, Thursday or Saturday. But not on a Monday. On a Monday it's old, and with chicken, old does not equal good. Most large-scale producers have had or do have a problem with salmonella, a bacteria that can cause severe food poisoning.

Most restaurants don't order or receive food on the day it's eaten. Despite best intentions, they have to work ahead. Because anything uneaten is kept for the next night, the chicken that wasn't eaten on Saturday is still sitting in the same juices it was on Monday.

Properly cooked and stored chicken shouldn't be a threat from salmonella, even on a Monday. It just smells that way when you open the bag. But someone, somewhere, may not be doing the right thing and you don't want to be the one to find out.

Don't order cooked oysters anytime

And particularly beware any raw or cooked oysters that are bought by the restaurant pre-opened. Need convincing? See chapter 1.

Buffet food is older than you think

Oh, it's an all-you-can-eat seafood buffet, is it? Well, along with the mounds of gangrenous prawns, possibly lethal oysters, botulism-laced terrines and poisonous washed-out-tasting lobsters are salads laced with listeria and desserts rich in staphylococcus. Why? Because all the same food was on the buffet yesterday; a few people probably sneezed on it, and while it still looks kind of fresh, the chef or hotel manager is desperately trying to make it last. How do I know? Because I've worked there.

Don't tip if there's a surcharge

If a restaurant has a surcharge, up to 15 per cent for

weekends and public holidays, keep the tip to yourself. The waiters will be on a decent penalty rate, or the owners are pocketing the surcharge themselves. Either way, the surcharge is a habit we, as diners, should discourage.

Avoid rum balls
Old cake. Buckets full of stale, horrid trimmings swept from the bench. You'd never touch those scraps and simply eat them, but mangle them up with melted chocolate, apricot jam and some kind of cheap and skanky rum essence, then roll them in coconut and you've got rum balls. Not recommended.

Some talent substitutes
The most common trick among talentless cooks is the simplest. Just make the food taste like snack food. Add some sugar, some extra salt, some monosodium glutamate (MSG, either natural or artificial) or the more recent panacea, truffle oil. Or add all those things. MSG and other glutamates exist in tomato sauce, mushrooms, seaweed, and a whole lot of other quite satisfying foods such as aged cheeses. Used well (think sushi, porcini risotto) they're superb, but used as a quick fix, the one-night stand of flavours leaves you with a sense of dissatis-faction, a feeling of being gastronomically robbed.

Truffle oil, the BO of restaurant perfumes, is a manu-factured product that has a mouth-filling feeling not dissimilar to MSG. It's like banana flavouring or artificial vanilla in that it's not a real flavour. Chefs who use it either can't buy good enough ingredients or they can't cook well enough to get by without adding fake flavours. What's most disappointing is that even the most expensive restaurants in the country do it.

Beware the truffle

Not just truffle oil, but truffle 'substitutes'. Chefs who wouldn't think of adding artificial rum essence to their food are, for some strange reason, happy to add 'truffle paste' or 'truffle extract'.

Real truffles, eaten fresh not preserved, are incredible things. That's *tuber melanosporum* – the black winter truffle – and *tuber magnatum pico* – the life-altering white winter truffle. The aroma, a compelling mix of earth, sex and death is more than just a little arousing. Other things, including that overrated, overpriced version of dirt, the summer truffle, are just over-hyped garbage being foisted on diners who think they're getting something good when they're not. What's wrong with fresh food, cooked properly? Excuse the kitchen French but it pisses me off that a country as bountiful as ours, one that should be helping to educate a new generation of diners, is merely cashing in on the hype of an ingredient that few people, including chefs, understand.

I adore truffles, but I also love top-quality fresh ingredients cooked so they taste of themselves. To avoid being duped and disappointed, unless you know and trust the restaurant, I generally advise against anything labelled 'truffle'.

Watch out for restaurants that use too much fruit with their meats

Fruit's the same as sugar: a mask for inferior cooking. It's pandering to our childhood love of anything sweet. Clever chefs use more acidic fruits with meats, but it's rare that any really nail it. About 300 years ago we invented a whole course for sweet fruit. Save it for dessert.

Regulars get better service

Do you like the idea of being treated like a restaurant critic? It's easy. Good places know their fiercest critics – and most ardent supporters – are their regular clients.

Being a familiar face will get you better service, a warmer welcome, better (and sometimes more) food, and a permanent place in the restaurateur's heart (unlike the reviewer). It's more important to show allegiance than to chase slightly better food elsewhere, because your local will take regulars' comments and complaints seriously.

Big tippers are treated better

We may be an egalitarian society, but if you want good treatment on your next visit, a generous tip is fondly remembered.

A high-scoring restaurant isn't necessarily better

I made a living out of scoring restaurants, and trust me, the thing that matters isn't always the score. Today is a casual day. I don't want the best wine list, the best space. I'm not prepared to pay for a view and in fact I just want pizza. Tomorrow I may want to get dressed up and lash out. Next week I may want something quick and local. Tonight I'll eat at a place that scores 13 out of 20, and love it. Rarely I might visit an 18 out of 20. I like to haunt a 16 out of 20 as often as money and circumstance allow, but only one out of the several that get that score in *The Good Food Guide*. Why? Because it suits me, my time in life, my needs.

Relying totally on the scores is silly. Like the best made movie, or the best theatre, sometimes a restaurant is simply not to your taste. Maybe you can't tell the difference between the food at a restaurant that scores 14 out of 20 and above. Great; you may be able to dine out regularly at places where you love the food and spend far less money. Maybe you're a real connoisseur, never happy with food at a place that scores less than 16 out of 20? Terrific, but I'll bet not all the restaurants at that level are your style.

That's the beauty of it. There are restaurants for everybody, at almost every budget. My favourite casual noodle house serves twelve dumplings for $7 – enough for a meal. It never once made *The Good Food Guide*. My favourite posh restaurant in the world cost me $400 just for the food. It has three Michelin stars. My favourite risotto is at home. The best roast pork I've eaten was at a mate's house, the finest cheese slurped as it ran down my face on the street in Italy, the best bread broken with friends, the greatest food experience in an area not known for prizing personal safety.

The best restaurant for you is one you like and can afford.

Being defensive is the best strategy

Defensive dining is the safest bet. Don't order dishes that sound odd, or sound like you won't like them. Don't order a lobster terrine just because you like lobster – for your tastes it could well have been mucked about with too much. Don't order much besides steak at a regional restaurant unless it has a good reputation. If an Aussie restaurant can cook anything, it should be able to cook steak (though in regional Australia ask for it rare if you want any residual moisture). Don't order steak at a fish restaurant, or expect much of a place that boasts 'curries, pasta and pizza'. Nobody can be an expert in every cuisine. Don't expect a Lebanese restaurant to do good paella, or a Spanish restaurant to do brilliant kofta. Use your commonsense and order what the restaurant is most likely to do well.

So you want it fast, cheap and great tasting – pick two

As Alan Benson, food photographer, former chef and one of my regular dining companions points out, food is rarely good, cheap and fast, though it can be two of the three. You can have a good fast pizza, but in this country it'll cost you about $20 (unlike Naples where it's closer to $8). You can get fast food that is reasonably cheap, but not great to eat. And you can get great-tasting cheap food that takes a bit of time to cook. It's admirable to look for all three, and I wish you luck.

Never trust a cab driver's dining recommendations

Taxidrivers, god love 'em, aren't the most cashed up or the savviest of diners. Mostly they want it cheap, fast, and they aren't so interested in how good it is. Asking a taxidriver about a good restaurant to take someone for a business lunch or anniversary is like asking them about immigration or politics. Sure they'll have an opinion, but it's probably not based on anything sound. Trusting them on dining is like letting them run the country because they reckon they're the only ones that can.

In fairness, taxidrivers can usually point you towards a good pie. The only proper restaurants you can trust a taxidriver about, however, are Chinese restaurants recommended by Chinese expats and halal restaurants recommended by Pakistani drivers. But remember, if a taxi smells like the driver's just finished a fantastic meal, it's probably been cooked by his wife.

Cheap café bacon smells of fish

Boar taint. Eurrgghh. Just the term has me shaking involuntarily. About 10 per cent of all non-castrated male pigs raised in Australia have this hormonal stink. More, if you ask me. It's a boy thing; pungent, socky, feral and funky — one report I read compares one of the hormones to the smell of mothballs. It's as bad as it sounds, but seldom talked about. Shame, because have you ever noticed a café's bacon smelling of fish? Or that the ham you bought has a bit of a whiff about it other than the smoke it's been brushed with, sorry, the smoke it's been dipped in? That's boar taint. Animals with this hormonal tang are usually sent for production as smallgoods rather than as fresh meat. But you can be unlucky.

Bread is the new rice

Western-style restaurants have finally cottoned on. Cheap Asian restaurants can charge $15 for a main course for many reasons, but one reason is that they also charge $4 a head for rice, when it's only a couple of dollars for a kilo bag and unlike most food it expands in both size and weight when cooked.

Maybe they've seen this potential for profit (or let's

blame those dreary Atkins dieters), because many western restaurants have now put a price tag on the most basic staple: bread. They may serve it with dukkah and bad olive oil (God help us all), or labne, or some dips, but it's just bread for crying out loud, something to mop up sauces. It should come for free, and not be cleared until after the main courses.

Melted cheese makes everything taste good

The toasted cheese sandwich. God love it. I sure do. Even commercially produced cheddar, which sweats in bags and creates a formaldehyde taint, one that isn't ripened naturally but is available at any corner store or supermarket, makes great toasted sandwiches. Melted cheese just rocks.

So if you're a chef with frozen seafood, a restaurateur who wants to use up flaccid vegetables, or if you're relatively untrained and put in charge of a kitchen, what do you do? Put cheese on things. On anything. Mornay sauce to disguise a pungent, sulphurous lobster? Oh, why not. Macaroni cheese in a fine diner? Go on then. Cheesy pasta, cheese on seafood, cheese with tinned pineapple, or with ham to hide the boar taint? Bad Mexican restaurants (is that tautology?) have known the power of molten *fromage* for years. So have bad Italian joints. If you put a sharp cheese on things, particularly if it's melted, it'll taste satisfying.

But melted cheese is just a bit too greasy, a bit too one dimensional, and it feels better if it's left for pizza or that weekend lunch with the Breville rather than used to obscure the watery flavour of frozen fish, the lack of complexity in a ragu, or the manky nature of the vegies.

January is the worst month for seafood

It's simple, really; fisherfolk have holidays. Yes, bad weather has an affect on what's in the market, but during January, particularly early January, just about the only fresh sea-food, and certainly the only affordable seafood, is farmed. Even then, the prices usually rise. That's okay, but paying $35 for a piece of farmed salmon at a restaurant, when you could be eating King George whiting or a piece of gold band snapper, is a bit disappointing. It won't hurt you, but instead, why not dip a line in the water yourself over the next holiday season.

How to tell if a restaurant special is special, or off

Specials, when I started work, were always made from food that was on the turn. It was the kitchen's way of shifting old food quickly because if you call something a special, it moves a hell of a lot faster than if it's on the menu. 'Special' might sound like it's cheap, or important, but most of the time it's just about off.

A real special is something bought in specially. And good restaurants these days do have real specials. The trick is to check the special against the menu. If there's fresh salmon on the menu, and fresh salmon on the specials list, don't order it. If there's tuna on the specials list, but no tuna on the menu, it probably means it's quite special.

There are a few don'ts. Don't order from a 'specials' list that is laminated, or on grease-splattered paper. Don't trust a waiter who can't tell you what the special tastes like – good restaurants offer a sample to staff so they can try it, but the dodgy ones just hope their spotty, ill-trained floor staff can sell it untried. Don't order a turkey special in

January. Don't trust anything called 'fantasia' or 'treat' or 'chef's daily special' or 'chef's special sauce' as they all just mean nobody is quite sure what's in the food. Anything called 'surprise' is going to surprise you a few hours after you've eaten, and not in a good way.

The chef is infallible

Take it from someone who had to grumble for a living, if you have reason to complain it may be met with derision. Don't give up, but just remember, chefs think they're infallible and hate to admit they could ever make a mistake, especially to a customer during the heat of service. Complaining is never a great thing to have to do, but it's how a restaurant deals with it that really counts. Beware the sent-back steak; if you wanted it cooked more it's probably been stomped on, beaten, rubbed on the chef's privates and dunked in the deep fryer before it returns, dry and rubbery, to your plate.

How to complain

Have a quiet word to the waiter about any issue, trying not to disturb the diners on your table – after all, they're out for a good time. If that doesn't work, excuse yourself, get up from your seat and take the manager to one side to discuss your grievance. Explain what's wrong, and how you think it can be fixed. Not liking the wine or a dish if it's as described on the menu is not something they have to act on, but they may.

Don't expect results. I once complained about overcooked fish at one of Melbourne's most famous French restaurants only to have the waiter return to the table, flicking the end of the offending fish. 'Zee chef and I eff bose tasted zees dish,' he said with true Gallic scorn. 'And zere is nussink wronk weeth eet,' handing the fish back to me to eat after they'd already had a chomp on it. If it wasn't for the defamation laws I'd tell you which restaurant.

What have you got for vegetarians?
How about disdain? Or contempt?

Vegetarians who spend any time eating out don't need to be told that the only thing a chef has for them is a mouthful of spite. Most chefs don't understand vegetarian food (it takes more skill to do vego than most meat cookery) and they don't take it seriously. These cowboys take all the prepared vegetables from the fridge and throw them together with acidic tomato puree and call it dinner. But it's not always the restaurant's fault.

The thing about vegetarians that really pisses chefs off is that they're so contrary; an enormous number of people become vegetarian only when they arrive at the restaurant. They don't tell the restaurant on the phone when they book, assuming – like righteous folk the world over – that everybody has the same hang-ups. When I worked in a function kitchen we'd always ask the organisers, more than once, about dietary requirements. And then we'd make an extra five or six dishes ready for all those who decided to become vegetarian after they'd sat down for dinner.

Arriving at a restaurant without telling them of your needs is not just disrespectful, it's plain stupid. Chefs cook food the same way people do at home – preparing every-thing ready in the hours before mealtimes, mostly to cook it at the last minute. If they don't know what you'll need, they don't prepare anything. When an out-of-the-ordinary request comes in, when fifty other people have also ordered, you'll get whatever sludge they can find in a hurry. Decide you're a vego, ring them ahead and you may well get special treatment.

The good news, at least in Australia, is that many top-end restaurants cook some of the best vegetarian food anywhere. Some even have separate vegetarian menus, and the dishes are so sublime you may want to become vegetarian at short notice.

Great Australian produce is often a furphy

It's not just the chefs, it's the producers and the suppliers. And the media who are sucked in by them. But when someone says Australia has the best produce in the world you know they're lying, or they're trying to sell you something. Sure, I'd like to pander to our cultural insecurity, but the reality is that countries such as France, Italy, China and even the UK in many instances, have better produce than us. Anybody who's travelled can tell you that.

Bad customers get bad service

The worst customers – the grumpy, grizzly, condescending ones – tend to get the worst service. The best service seems to be reserved for polite diners (Chinese restaurants excluded).

'Sparkling, please . . . and why don't you stiff us in the process?'

I tried. I pushed restaurants and diners alike, but still you can dine many, many times, especially in the cities, before you're offered tap water. Some restaurants don't even pay for their mineral water (it's brand positioning) and we all know how little it costs by the case, so why do they stiff us for about $10 a bottle? Because we let them.

Expensive fitouts cost money

World-class fitouts and designer lights are great to have, but they come at a cost; at least part of your bill covers the seat you're sitting on, the water glimpses and the Florence Broadhurst wallpaper. That's one reason why modest Asian joints and cafés can be such great comparative value.

If you want to be hated, ask for changes to what's on the menu

Good restaurants have a reason for the way they put things together on the menu. They've thought about it, and reckon those combinations will work best. If you change things around, you risk not only damaging the chef's delicate ego, but also mucking up the seamless way a good kitchen operates during service. Your meal will take longer, it'll be prepared with a hint of bile (and maybe a touch of spit) and you'll probably slow up everybody else's meal too. Some chefs think, rightly or wrongly, that if you don't like their food the way it was intended, you should just fuck off and eat somewhere else.

Coffee is the most expensive item on the menu

It costs a fair bit to put food on a plate. I buy duck legs for $10 retail, but can get them cooked by a professional, in a restaurant, served with sauce and garnishes, and with someone to wash up, for $25 or $30. Duck is messy, time consuming, and while I do cook it at home, most people probably don't. The mark-up is fair. But coffee is the great rip-off of our times. The grower gets about 8¢ a cup, at most, usually less. It costs about 60¢ to make a flat white and it can cost up to $12 to buy the sucker in a restaurant. Petit fours, those little sweets that come with it, are often the excuse. But if all you want is a coffee, in posh places there's no choice, the petit fours are rammed down your credit card.

Now the 60¢ to make coffee is based on organic milk (so rare it's virtually extinct) and top-shelf coffee (likewise). It costs less to make a ristretto or short black – milk is actually more expensive than the coffee most of the time. If you use cheap coffee – or like some restaurants, get it for free as an act of brand placement – then anything more than $2.50 is a serious mark-up. As cafés charge $3, a posh restaurant, with all their overheads, should be able to charge $4. Or throw it in with the $150 menu and show a little hospitality, you greedy bastards. And while you're at it, make it properly why don't you – most restaurant coffee tastes like the liquid you'd get when you clean out the machine.

Restaurants have the airline attitude to both tea and coffee – if it's warm, and kind of brown coloured, then they think it's okay. It's not okay, and as consumers it's up to us to force them to change.

The best restaurant is ...
- *local* – close to your home or perhaps your work. That way you can go when you're drinking and don't want to drive, and you can go there regularly.
- *affordable,* so you can enjoy it often.

- *somewhere you feel comfortable.* Each to their own – as I often think, if it's too loud, or too dark, then I'm too old (for *that* restaurant, at least).
- *serving food you like to eat and wines you want to drink.* Simple really.
- *somewhere that makes you feel loved* – and that's different for you than it is for me.
- *flawed.* Like choosing a life partner, you won't find happiness by seeking flaws in a restaurant; rather, rejoice in their strengths.

How to dine like royalty on kitchenhand wages

Most of us mere mortals can't afford to eat at Australia's best restaurants very often, but if you can spend $200 wisely in our world-class eateries, it's far more likely to be something you'll remember in ten years than spending the equivalent amount on a service for the car.

Some restaurateurs might not like the table that doesn't 'order up', but most should be happy to have bums on seats early in the week, especially at lunchtime. And remember, the price you pay for the food when wages, rent, and all the other costs are taken into consideration is still too cheap for a product that is handcrafted from raw, moving through research, development, production and marketing in a matter of hours. Here are a few tips to squeeze the most from a restaurant when you're not as flush as you'd like to be.

- *Listen to advice.* A review or a personal recommendation is the best way to ensure the place is your style. Don't just go on the score if using a review; read the words to see if it will suit your needs.

- *Visit early in the week* so you're not taking a table that the restaurateur can make heaps more money on – that way you'll usually get far better service as the waiters have more time for you. (This also avoids the all too common surcharge on weekends and public holidays.)
- *Never, ever, order mineral water, coffee, tea or a side dish* – that's where many restaurants have stupid mark-ups.
- *Don't have a pre-dinner drink.* BYO if possible and order wine by the glass if you feel you can survive on just one or two.
- *Share everything.* That way, even a two-course dinner can feel nearly as good as a full tasting menu.
- *Use special offers,* be it pre-theatre, lunch deals, or set-priced menus, particularly those that may include a glass of wine. A good chef will always try to cook like an angel, including dishes or menus at more earthly prices. Set menus, even when they're not the cheapest option, are usually priced on the punter's side – less wastage for the kitchen means they can afford to give you more for your dollar.
- *Never allow yourself to feel intimidated* or inferior for not ordering the most expensive items on the menu. A good restaurant offers a warm welcome to everybody, and if they treat you right when you're not spending, you're much more likely to go back when you're next cashed up. What's more, they never know who the next reviewer for *The Sydney Morning Herald* may be.
- *Take notes.* My mum does it, and she's found that the service can improve. She scans the room, jots a few things on her shopping list, pulls the list from her bag once more when the entrees arrive and rattles the

restaurant. The best thing that can happen if lots of people start to take notes is that restaurants will never know who is reviewing them and who isn't. It's better for you, and better for the critics who are trying to help you, too.

- *Remember them when the tax refund cheque or bonus arrives.* While a good restaurant can make you feel loved when you're not flush, the same place should be able to move your world in a far greater way when you're in the money. A pre-dinner drink, some salad, a dessert wine and a full menu can all take the normally great meal to some other, more stratospheric height.